BULLYING

BULLYING
A Spiritual Crisis

Ronald Hecker Cram

CHALICE PRESS

ST. LOUIS, MISSOURI

Biblical quotations, unless otherwise noted, are from the *New Revised Standard Version Bible*, copyright 1989, Division of Christian Education of the National Council of the Churches of Christ in the United States of America. Used by permission. All rights reserved.

Excerpts from *The New Jerusalem Bible*, copyright 1985 by Darton, Longman & Todd, Ltd., and Doubleday, a division of Bantam Doubleday Dell Publishing Group, Inc. Used by permission.

Cover photo: Skjold Photographs
Cover and interior design: Elizabeth Wright

This book is printed on acid-free, recycled paper.

Visit Chalice Press on the World Wide Web at
www.chalicepress.com

10 9 8 7 6 5 4 3 2 1   03 04 05 06 07 08

Library of Congress Cataloging–in–Publication Data

Cram, Ronald Hecker.
  Bullying : a spiritual crisis / Ronald Hecker Cram.— 1st ed.
      p. cm.
  Includes bibliographical references.
  ISBN 0-8272-0234-2 (pbk. : alk. paper)
  1. Violence—Religious aspects—Christianity. I. Title.
  BT736.15.C73 2003
  261.8'32—dc21
                                                          2003008922

Printed in the United States of America

For Susan

Contents

Acknowledgments

To Abingdon Press, for permission to quote Carol Lakey Hess, *Caretakers of Our Common House: Women's Development in Communities of Faith* (1997), 35.

To the Continuum International Publishing Group, to quote from Marjorie Suchocki, *The Fall to Violence* (1994), 144.

To the Editor of *Conversations*, for permission to quote David Hollenbach, S. J., "Is Tolerance Enough? The Catholic University and the Common Good," n. 13, spring 1996: 8.

To Cornell University Press for permission to quote from W. R. Johnson, *Momentary Monsters: Lucan and His Heroes*. Copyright 1987 by Cornell University.

To the Crossroad Publishing Company for permission to quote from Gil Bailie, *Violence Unveiled: Humanity at the Crossroads* (1995).

To the Editor, Director of Creative Services at Agnes Scott College, for permission to quote from the article by Robert Coles, "The Moral Life of Children," *Agnes Scott Alumnae Magazine*, Fall 1989: 16.

To Wm. B. Eerdmans Publishing Co., for permission to quote from J. Denny Weaver, *The Nonviolent Atonement* (2001), pp. 52, 225.

To HarperCollins Publishers, for brief quotations (pp. 343–44) from *God for Us: The Trinity and Christian Life* by Catherine Mowry LaCugna, copyright © 1991 by Catherine Mowry LaCugna, reprinted by permission of HarperCollins Publishers, Inc.

To HarperCollins Publishers, for single sentence quotation (p. 446) from *Catholicism, Completely Revised and Updated* by Richard P. McBrien, copyright © 1994 by Richard P. McBrien, reprinted with permission of HarperCollins Publishers, Inc.

To HarperCollins Publishers, for single sentence quotation [p. 19] from *To Know as We Are Known* by Parker J. Palmer, copyright © 1983, 1993 by Parker J. Palmer, reprinted with permission of Harper Collins Publishers, Inc.

To The Johns Hopkins University Press, for permission to quote Toril Moi, "The Missing Mother: The Oedipal Rivalries of René Girard," *Diacritics*, v. 12, p. 22; René Girard, *Violence and the Sacred* (Baltimore, 1977), p. 259; René Girard, *The Scapegoat* (Baltimore, 1989), p. 42.

To the Editor of the *Journal of Liberal Religion*, for permission to quote from all published articles by Ronald Hecker Cram.

To Morehouse Publishing, for permission to quote from *Victimization: Examining Christian Complicity*, copyright 1996 by Christine Gudorf. Reprinted by permission of Morehouse Publishing, Harrisburg, PA.

To Markus Muller, for permission to quote from "Interview with René Girard," *Anthropoetics*, June 1996, p. 6.

To Oxford University Press, for permission to quote an extract from page 72 of *The Idea of the Holy* by Rudolf Otto, translated by John W. Harvey (1923).

To Doubleday and Company, a division of Random House, Inc., for permission to quote from Peter Berger and Thomas Luckmann, *The Social Construction of Reality* (1967).

To the Editor of *Religious Education*, for permission to quote from all published articles written by Ronald Hecker Cram.

To T. & T. Clark, Ltd., for permission to quote Eberhard Jüngel, *God as the Mystery of the World: On the Foundation of the Theology of the Crucified One in the Dispute between Theism and Atheism*, translated by Darrell L. Guder (Edinburgh, Scotland, 1983), p. 104.

To Desmond Tutu, "Justice, Memory and Reconciliation," p.4, accessed February 1, 2002. Used with permission by Desmond Tutu, taken from the commencement address at the University of Toronto.

To the Regents of the University of California for permission to use material published in Nel Noddings, *Caring: A Feminine Approach to Ethics and Moral Education*, copyright © 1984.

To the University of Massachusetts Press to quote from Susan Ford Wiltshire, *Public and Private in Vergil's Aeneid* (Amherst, 1989), p. 83.

To the University of Texas Press to quote from *The Dialogic Imagination: Four Essays* by Michael Holquist, translated by Caryl Emerson and Michael Holquist, copyright © 1981.

To Elie Wiesel, for permission to quote from his 1997 DePaul commencement address, "Learning and Respect: A Challenge to Graduates."

For excerpts from *Night* by Elie Wiesel, translated by Stella Rodway. Copyright © 1960 by MacGibbon & Kee. Copyright © renewed 1988 by The Collins Publishing Group. Reprinted by permission of Hill and Wang, a division of Farrar, Straus and Giroux, LLC.

Preface

Since the 1983 Norwegian Ministry of Education's nationwide anti-bullying campaign, bullying has become a serious area of inquiry and debate in Europe, Australia, and more recently the United States. The tragic events surrounding Columbine High School in Colorado and the destruction of the World Trade Center towers have intensified the public's attention to violence in general, and bullying in particular. The first significant empirical study of bullying that appeared in *The Journal of the American Medical Association* in April 2001 (reported on widely by the media) signaled a growing urgency and concern within the academic community to provide research that could serve as the foundation for informed practice.[1]

Yet while public interest and research attention around the globe have begun to focus in intentional ways on the issue of bullying, virtually no ongoing research on bullying exists within the field of Christian religious education. But the church or the parish is exactly where the topic of bullying needs to be talked about and explored. Christian religious education is concerned with instruction in the content of faith only insofar as that instruction invites reflection about appropriate and life-giving practices of life together in a pluralistic world. It is the thesis of this book that bullying is an indication of spiritual crisis expressed outwardly as a desire to be in relation with another person or persons—but with the opposite result. As a practical theologian with specific interest in Christian religious education, I believe it is not enough to rely on sociological and psychological research in my exploration of bullying. These are important resources, but valuable only as they are brought into conversation with Christian theological resources. The discussion of bullying is fundamentally an issue of social justice that arises from Christian theological conviction about a relational ontology embodied by the Triune God for and with us. A critique of bullying arises from a Christian understanding of who God is for us. A constructive alternative to bullying arises from a Christian understanding of the Trinity.

This book is intended to be an exploration in practical theology on the theme of bullying. It is hoped that interest and debate that may arise from the reading of this text will result in further experiments of critical reflection and action for the common good. In the last analysis, it is not so much important that the reader agrees or disagrees with my perspective as that conversation about bullying begin to take place in churches, schools, workplaces, and homes. I write this book as a privileged and white Catholic male during a period of great national interest in the ideas of retaliation, in a time of simplistic division of humanity into good and evil, secret keeping, collateral damage (particularly Afghan, Palestinian, and Iraqi women and children), and "terrorism." This book is an artifact or case study of the contemporary global culture of violence as well as a contribution to Christian religious education.

The first chapter of this book focuses on the roots of violence. This is not intended to be an exhaustive treatment of the fall to violence by humanity, but a heuristic exploration of the interplay of human relatedness and human sin. Chapter 2 presents a case study of a man who was bullied as a child—who looks back on the experience and shows the consequences for adult religious self-reflection. This case study was part of a larger research project begun in 1996 that was given administrative support by Columbia Theological Seminary. This particular case was paradigmatic of the many interviews of adults who had been bullied as children conducted over a period of five years. Not only did the man interviewed give permission to print this case, but he encouraged me to do so—with the hope that others might be helped. For this act of moral courage, I am enormously grateful.

Chapter 3 develops the theme of bullying as a spiritual crisis, and chapter 4 suggests various concrete practices of empathy (a crucial antidote to bullying) in which Christians may engage—in the home, workplace, school, and church or local parish. Chapter 5 contains a working bibliography for future study and practice.

This book may be used in many ways. For the university or seminary student, the book may provide a preliminary way to enter into a theological and educational discussion of this very important issue. Extensive endnotes are provided for scholarly engagement and research. For the parent or caregiver of children, starting with the case study may be the best choice, moving to practical ways of practicing justice and empathy. For the parish principal, teachers, Sunday school teachers, and other religious educators, the resource annotations and practices of empathy may be of greatest help. This book can be used in many ways, depending on the needs and interests of the reader.

My work on the topic of bullying had its theological origins in the scholarship of Catherine Mowry LaCugna. She was extremely encouraging to me in the early stages of my work, and her untimely death in 1997 was a great loss to all of us who work in the area of theology. She took what can be a dreadfully parched topic, the Trinity, and revealed an authentically Christian understanding of human relations that arises from the praise of God.

To Carlos Cardoza-Orlandi, Peter Gilmour, Rita Guare, Beth Johnson, Gerone Lockhart, Roberta Nelson, Kathleen O'Connor, Don Ratcliff, Marcia Y. Riggs, Henry Simmons, Christine Roy Yoder, for giving comment on various sections of this book, I extend collegial thanks. To students at Columbia Theological Seminary in Decatur, Georgia, who have taken my course *The Spiritual Lives of Children;* members of The Council of Churches and Synagogues in Stamford, Connecticut; members of the Board of Directors of The Religious Education Association; peers in The Association of Professors and Researchers in Education; Clive Erricker and Cathy Ota (who gave frank and needed comment in the initial steps of research); Andrea Lerner and other good friends in the Liberal Religious Educators Association who gave good feedback to my 1999 Fahs Lecture; the many laity who engaged in special programs and classes led by me on the topic of bullying; my diverse parish, The Catholic Shrine of the Immaculate Conception in Atlanta, Georgia; and Columbia Theological Seminary I express deep gratitude. I am particularly grateful to the editor of the journal *Religious Education,* Theodore Brelsford, and the editor of the *Journal of Liberal Religion,* Kenneth A. Olliff, for permission to quote extensively from articles I previously published. While this book is in a real way an act of interdisciplinary collaboration with many conversation partners, its limitations are my own. My deepest appreciation is given to Jon L. Berquist of Chalice Press for his encouragement and direction. To Susan Hecker Cram, dearest of friends, lover of children, healer of the wounds of injustice and oppression, I humbly dedicate this book.

Ronald Hecker Cram
Easter Sunday
New Orleans

CHAPTER 1

Violence and Christian Life

For several years I have been teaching Sunday morning classes in local churches and parishes on the topic of bullying. These classes are very well attended, because concerned parents and caregivers are confused by and concerned about the rise of violence among children in the United States. One Sunday morning a father in his mid-thirties brought his ten-year-old daughter to one of my classes.

The child was dreadfully uncomfortable—not so much because she was the only child in a room filled with adults, but more from the discomfort of a troubled heart. It was very clear that she was so upset that she barely noticed anyone other than her father. As the class began, the child's nervous father raised a quaking hand. I invited him to speak to the whole group. He began tentatively and with difficulty, "My daughter is afraid to go to school. Nobody seems to care. Teachers and administrators aren't helping us—they don't know what to do. I don't understand why a group of older girls would want to threaten my daughter, and I'm afraid of what might happen. I pray to God to stop the violence, and that doesn't work. I wonder if God cares at all. Friends tell me not to worry,

1

that the bullying will go away in time, that 'kids will be kids.' But the bullying is not going away; it is getting worse and worse. We feel helpless. Please help us. We don't know what to do." This agonized father and daughter came to a local church school class on Sunday morning raising questions that many persons are asking, questions that deserve to be discussed within the context of a Christian faith.

This father and daughter invite us to ask two very important (and very uncomfortable) questions: What is bullying, and why should Christian people take bullying seriously? In order to begin to answer these two important questions, we must turn to our deepest beliefs and understandings of God and of human beings. In the popular press, this is not the starting point of the public discussion about bullies! A theological understanding of bullying has been ignored in the public discussion of this sensitive and important social issue. For Christian people, violence is a matter of enormous theological importance.

By entering into an examination of violence, Christians are confronted with some of the most important questions of Christian theology: What does it mean to be human? Who is God? What is the meaning of the crucifixion? and How shall we live together in the world? In other words, by examining the spiritual crisis of bullying, we find ourselves in the presence of some of the most important questions in the mystery of Christian life.

Violence is something with which every Christian must come to terms. After all, Jesus was killed in an act of violence, and what we believe about Jesus shapes our understanding of the meaning, nature, and purposes of the Christian life. Our faith in Jesus is born in violence, whether we consciously think about this fact or not. This chapter begins with an overview of our relation with God, ourselves, others, and the earth. The basic themes of doxology and sin guide our initial discussion of the way in which our relation with God shapes our entire Christian life. This rather simple discussion leads us, however, to more complicated issues and themes. Did God send Jesus to earth in order to forgive human sin? Paul, our dominant biblical theologian, was writing in a particular culture at a particular time. How did Paul's understanding of the life and death of Jesus (what we call in theology "atonement") shape our understanding of sin and forgiveness? How we Christians make sense out of the death of Jesus leads us to the last, and perhaps most important, questions of this chapter. Where was God at the time of the crucifixion of Jesus, and where is God speaking God's good news to us today?

Violence, Doxology, and Sin: Relational Starting Points

Bullying is an act of violence. As curious as it may seem, the origin of violence is found in the innate human desire to be in relation with another person. Is this not a good thing, to be in relation with another person? Indeed, the desire to be in relation with another person lies at the very heart of what it means to be human. To desire to be in relation with another person is part of what it means to be created in the image of God. God has created human beings to be in relation with Godself, to be in communion with God. God has created human beings to be in relation with God and with one another. From this perspective, there is no "I" apart from a "Thou" or "We." Persons in the northern Natal in South Africa greet one another with the words, "*Sawu bona.*" These words mean, "I see you." The proper reply to "*Sawu bona*" is, "*Sikhona.*" This reply means, "I am here." Reflecting on this greeting and response, organizational theory expert Peter Senge writes, "'The order of the exchange is important: until you see me, I do not exist. It's as if when you see me, you bring me into existence."[1]

The desire to be in relation with the other, a desire written on the human heart by God, can be life-giving. Communion with another person has the potential for joy, peace, safety, hope, and love. The desire to be in relation with the other, a desire written on the human heart by God, can be life-robbing. Communion with another person has the potential for agony, war, insecurity, despair, and hate. Violence as a form of relationship is not rational. It is not rational to harm another person physically or psychologically. Violence is not rational, but it is always relational.

We forget sometimes that the desire to be in relation with the other is the basis of all violence. How odd this sounds to our ears at first! Common sense tells us that violence is the desire to end relation with others—not to be in relation with others. On closer examination, however, we begin to understand how violence is a way of being in relation with the other person.

The desire to be in relation with another person, a gift from God, is a deep part of what it means to be human. The desire to be in relation with another person is a deep yearning. To be in relation with another person in a spirit of doxology, however, has a different consequence than to be in relationship with another person in a spirit of sin. What is doxology? What is sin?

Doxology and Sin

Think of doxology and sin as two sides of a coin we will call "relationship." Doxology means the praise of God. Doxology calls us to acts of justice and peace. Theologian Catherine Mowry LaCugna has written that doxology includes "everything that promotes fullness of humanity, that builds up relationships based on charity and compassion, and glorifies God."[2]

Sin, on the other hand, is the negation (or opposite) of doxology. Sin is everything that the praise of God is not. LaCugna has written that sin "is the absence of praise."[3] Correctly, LaCugna places her definition of sin within the context of relation with others. "Sin is the absence of right relationship, whether it is manifested in our relationships with each other (relationships of exploitation), to ourselves (egotism in both its forms: self-denigration and self-inflation), to the world (relationships of waste, consumerism, and destruction), or to God (the worship of false gods)."[4] Were there no such thing as human freedom, there would be no such thing as sin.

Sin is a verb. Sin is the desire to be in communion with the other but without that communion reflecting the praise of God. Sin is the desire to be in communion with the other but in all the wrong ways—in the ways that bring hate, destruction, and death. Violence is not a fundamental rejection of God's gift of relationality. In fact, violence is not a fundamental rejection of the desire to be in relation with the other person, which God has given all persons as a gift. Violence is sin. Violence is a way of being in relation with others, often including God, but in a misguided and destructive manner.

Viewed in this way, violence is a pattern of sinning that seeks to negate the other in futile expression to find relation (even to find God). The person who seeks to relate by means of violence to others is most of all a tragic figure on a positive religious quest (to be in relation with others and with God) whose futile end is the absence of doxological relation. Said another way, the positive religious quest to be in relation with others is also the quest of violence and of violation. But to seek relation with others by means of violence gives persons the exact opposite of that which they seek. The person who seeks relation through violence inevitably ends up isolated and alone. It is little wonder that sociologist Mark Juergensmeyer has concluded that religion can become a breeding ground for violence.[5] The religious dimensions of sin are not to be ignored. Sin and doxology are simply different sides of the same coin.

To be in relation with the other in a spirit of doxology, one comes to be increasingly drawn to the mystery of the other person, who has been created in the image of God. A spirit of doxology, enlivened by a spirit of mystery and humility, draws us naturally and quietly to gratitude and wonder of the other—and of ourselves. If a relationship with another is guided by a spirit of doxology, dignity and worth are afforded not only the other person but ourselves as we are transformed by love and become more fully respectful of the God who is with us, in us, and through us.

To be in relation with the other in a spirit of sin is an act of dehumanization for both the self and the other. Rather than being drawn to mystery and humility at the presence of God in the other, the other is reduced to a "thing." Philosopher Simone Weil understands this movement from humanization to dehumanization as *force*. She writes that force is "that *x* that turns anybody who is subjected to it into a *thing*."[6]

By turning the other into a thing, an act of the sin-guided religious imagination, one begins the pain-filled process of becoming a thing oneself. The desire to be in relation with the other person, a gift from God, continues to draw us to the other. This desire to be in relation with the other cannot be quenched easily, perhaps not at all. But sin misdirects doxology's life-giving resources.

To affirm the life of the "genuine other" with concern and a willingness to participate in the life of the genuine other is not only a manifestation of doxology in a person's life but also an affirmation of who God is for us in the world. Our relationships with ourselves, with others, and *with God* are at stake.

To turn another person into a thing has the inevitable result of turning ourselves into a thing and of turning God into a thing. God, who is *no-thing*, is negated in this sinful process. The negation of God is idolatry. To turn God or one who is created in God's image into a thing is a form of self-destructive violence. To be in relation with a God whom we have turned into a thing is to be in relation with nothing that is life-giving. Since we cannot know ourselves and others apart from God, the act of negating the other as created in the image of God results in alienation from the other, alienation from the self, and alienation from God—all at the same time.

A matrix of "things" lured by the inner God-given desire to be in relation with the other may be characterized as hell. The space of violence is a place of sin characterized by alienation and loneliness—the very opposites of what is desired. It is a space of force in which the destruction of the other becomes the only way to be in relation with the other, and the destruction of self the only logical outcome of being in relation to a self who has turned God into a thing. In this inversion of doxology, one can be in relation with oneself only by engaging in acts of violence against others—as well as oneself. Classicist W. R. Johnson has referred to this process of violence and hatred as "the rage to uncreate whatever is not itself."[7]

Such a rage, to uncreate the other, is an inadequate strategy for being in relation with the other. It is not possible to imagine a more fundamental spiritual crisis. One knows at the deepest (unconscious) levels that one has been created to be in relation with others. Yet the only way one knows how to be in relation with the other is through acts of violence. But instead of bringing a lasting relation with the other, violence gives only episodic, fleeting, and sporadic experiences of relation. The desire to be in relation with the other person becomes so intense, so powerful, that violence is increased. Perhaps, we think, if we increase the level of violence, our relation with the other person may remain longer, be more permanent? Alas! The very method used to establish relation with the other becomes so powerful in its fury that it permanently eliminates the other. All that remains is the rage-filled self, which begins in time to turn in on itself—frequently with self-destructive consequences. Even the self, at this point, can be in relation with the self only through the medium of violence.

The Context of our Relation with Others

Is this desire to be in relation with the other, including with God, to be understood in terms that are isolated from social location? This is not at all the case. To exist means to exist in relation with others *within social context*. Our drive toward relationship begins in infancy. Human development researcher Urie Bronfenbrenner has outlined an approach to understanding the growth of children that may help clarify the person within context. Bronfenbrenner's "ecological systems theory" invites us to begin by taking seriously the child's psychological and biological makeup. But he does not stop there. Bronfenbrenner continues his approach to understanding the child in context as the child in relation with others in such settings as the household, school, playground, Sunday school, and neighborhood. Bronfenbrenner calls these contexts the child's *microsystem*.

The microsystem is part of a larger system called the *mesosystem*. The mesosystem is concerned with the interdependent relationships between the various contexts of the microsystem. For example, if a child experiences violence in the home as the primary way of being in relation with another person, this pattern of relation will have implications not only within the household but for the other contexts of the child's everyday life as well. For example, making friends on the playground may be limited by the ways violence operates in the household.

The microsystem and the mesosytem are embedded within the *exosystem*. There are social, economic, religious, and political systems into which a child is born. The child does not create these systems, but is invited through the process of socialization to learn how to move and "be" within these systems. A child in Atlanta may not know what capitalism is in its more complex explanations, but from the very beginning of life the child will understand the experience of having purchasing power or not having purchasing power. This could be reflected in the diet chosen by the caregiver, the quality of medical care, access to information—or being able to purchase a gum ball at the local grocery store or not.

Bronfenbrenner continues by suggesting that the systems discussed thus far are embedded within a *macrosystem*. The macrosystem includes those formal and informal rituals of everyday life, religious values, ceremonies, and customs that shape directly and indirectly the moral climate of the culture into which the child is born. The *chronosystem* is the last system that Bronfenbrenner discusses. *Chronos* means time. When we look at all the systems in interdependence—microsystem, mesosystem, exosystem, and macrosystem—we realize that these systems are not static, but that they change through time in response to the changes in each system. Change in the systems takes place in and through time. These changes have consequences for the ways in which the other systems interact. The chronosystem gives "the big picture" of the interdependent systems over time.[8]

Sometimes the question arises: Are relational patterns to be viewed from a social/systemic perspective, or are they to be viewed from an interpersonal and psychological perspective? Bronfenbrenner helps us overcome the trap of choosing one approach over the other. The social reality of the everyday life of the child is too complex to answer in a simplistic manner. Even a response such as "both-and" is not adequate for the complexity of the child in an ecological systems context.

A story of my relation with a little boy whom I taught during a summer religious education program may help clarify the connection between interpersonal relationships and the wider social context. Several years ago, I was working during the summer with poor urban children at a parish in Trenton, New Jersey. One of the children, a boy aged six, was already known as a person of great emotional and physical violence.

Seated in a circle on the floor, I was teaching a Bible story to my group of a dozen six- and seven-year-old children. We were having a grand time! I noticed out of the corner of my eye that the little boy was walking over to me. I invited him to join the group, and as I moved to make room for him in the circle—whap! I felt his small but powerful fist plunge into my chest. I was knocked over by the force of the blow, and lay gasping for air, unable to breathe. I remember that with pain searing through my chest, I looked up from the floor into his wide and expectant eyes. The child lingered for a moment, then walked away. Later that day, in conversation with other group leaders who knew the child well, I discovered that he came from an abusive family situation. The only way he knew how to be in relation with others was through physical violence. In a very real way, this was the only way this dear little boy knew to begin a conversation or relationship with me. When I did not strike him back, the group leaders told me, the little boy was utterly confused. "Why doesn't Mr. Cram like me?" he asked another leader later. By not striking back, I was not enacting the pattern of relationship that had been established in his taken-for-granted world of violence.

But we would be in error to conclude that the child's home was somehow isolated or unrelated to the wider social context. The child had moved only recently to the United States from Central America. It was because of the violence in his country of origin that he and his family had fled to the United States. Once in the United States his parents did not have the economic or social skills to make an adequate living. His father became depressed, withdrawn, and physically violent. When the father was arrested for trying to break into a neighborhood grocery store, the mother and child were left with no prospects for a better life.

The "layers" of social systems that impacted this young boy are almost too hard to imagine. Global patterns of political and social violence are systemically related to the violent encounter I had with him in the quiet safety of the local parish Bible study.

Child advocate and educator Jonathan Kozol, in his book *Amazing Grace: The Lives of Children and the Conscience of a Nation*[9] reflects on the impact of the prison system on households in New York City. When a parent or parents are incarcerated, children in poverty have few opportunities to break out of a system of social and economic violence. Gentle and sweet children, he reflects, are maimed and twisted by social patterns of violence much beyond their control.[10] Ninety-two percent of the prisoners at Rikers Island in the East River are black or Hispanic.[11] It costs $64,000 a year to keep an adult in prison at Rikers Island; $93,000 to house a young person on the nearby prison barge.[12] These monetary figures mean nothing until we begin to take into account the households disrupted by parents and caregivers who are incarcerated, until we realize the resources denied families, schools, and social agencies, and when the inherent racism of "lockdown" in the United States is understood.[13]

The child's taken-for-granted world is a powerful socializer. Capacities for the development and nurture of empathy may not be present adequately within the child's environment. Appropriate adult guidance may not be present. Opportunities for positive peer interactions may be few. While the origin of sin has perplexed theologians for centuries, the perpetuation of sin is not as difficult to chart. From a Christian perspective, doxology is more powerful and inherently life-giving than sin. At the same time, it is equally true that once cycles and systems of sin are established, they are very difficult forces to stop. Violence gives pleasure to the person, organization, or nation engaged in it—but only while violence acts as a vehicle of connection with the victim of violence. Yes, bullying can take place between individuals or groups of persons. Violence exists because it reaps pleasure from the relation it establishes, however perverse. Violence is establishment of relation with the other that results in the negation of relation with the other. In our times the practices of doxology are radical invitations to reorienting the inward life, as well as "*the world out beyond.*"[14] But this language is misguiding if we do not recognize the interplay between the personal and the social that occurs at conscious and unconscious levels.

Let us take as an example the story of the young boy who hit me in the chest as a way of being in relation with me. Much discussion today suggests it is possible for children to be born with a genetic predisposition to violence. While a genetic predisposition to violence ought not be confused with an inevitability of violent behavior, it is likely that if violence is practiced in the home or school as appropriate social behavior, the genetic predisposition may, in fact, be nurtured and reinforced. Let us imagine further that the child is growing up in a social and economic climate that presumes financial and social discrimination/oppression based on race and class. The interdependent interaction of these systems with home life and psychological/genetic predispositions again reinforces the validity of violence. Let us assume further that the child is growing up in a country that values violent and brutal military reaction and blind patriotism that includes the need to divide the world into those who are good and those who are evil. And let us continue by presuming that such a political and military defense system embodies a pattern of retaliation over time, so that violent national behavior habitually becomes taken for granted—perhaps even sacred.

In such a hypothetical scenario, it would be inappropriate to deny the importance of taking into account psychological and genetic data. Parents and caregivers know that a child's personality is very much in evidence by age two—some attest even earlier. But it would be equally inappropriate to deny the social, political, and economic systems that reinforce public and private behavior and values. Bronfenbrenner helps us remember that the child is a person born into a multiplicity of reinforcing systems. What sociologists Peter L. Berger and Thomas Luckmann have called the processes of primary and secondary socialization are helpful ways of further clarifying the ecological systems theory of Bronfenbrenner. In Berger and Luckmann's insightful book on the process of socialization, *The Social Construction of Reality: A Treatise in the Sociology of Knowledge*, they write,

> Primary socialization is the first socialization an individual undergoes in childhood, through which he becomes a member of society. Secondary socialization is any subsequent process that inducts an already socialized individual into new sectors of the objective world of his society.[15]

Before a child can speak or even walk, her taken-for-granted world has entered her behavior patterns, thinking patterns, and sense of self in relation with others. It is very likely that by age five the child has already learned the basic cultural, political, economic, religious, gender, and racial/ethnic values of society. No wonder religious educator Parker Palmer has said that "education would not be necessary if things were as they seem."[16]

Our earliest understandings of religion often reinforce dominant cultural understandings of violence. This is particularly true for many Christian traditions, which trace their origins back to the life, execution, and resurrection of Jesus. Many Christian children and adults are taught that God required the death of Jesus in order to take away sin. But this commonplace understanding of the relation of God, Jesus, and sin may harbor implicit cultural values about abuse and violence that misinterpret the meaning of the execution of Jesus altogether.

The Meaning of the Execution of Jesus

Within much of the history of Christianity is an assumption that Jesus died for our sins (satisfaction atonement). In many Christian communities of faith, this assumption is taken for granted and unquestioned even today. But for theologian J. Christiaan Beker, the execution of Jesus on a cross by crucifixion "is not God's curse but the redemptive center of God's judgment and love for a lost world."[17] This is congruent with much of Pauline theology. Yet it is also possible to see the language of satisfaction atonement in Paul as well. Could both perspectives be articulated in the Pauline writings? If both views are present, why?

While there is no indication that early Christian communities uniformly linked the crucifixion of Jesus with forgiveness of human sin, Paul insisted that God's love for the world and God's judgment of human sin were resolved in the death of Jesus on the cross. In the letter to the Romans, Paul contends that "when we were still helpless, at the appointed time, Christ died for the godless. You could hardly find anyone ready to die even for someone upright; though it is just possible that, for a really good person, someone might undertake to die. So it is proof of God's own love for us, that Christ died for us while we were still sinners" (Rom. 5:6–8, *The New Jerusalem Bible*).[18]

Certainly, within the larger cultural context of Paul, the interpretation of the death of Jesus as a sacrificial act demanded by God for the forgiveness of human sin is understandable. There was a need to make sense out of the death of Jesus in a way that answered questions from Jewish scholars,[19] but the interpretation of the death of Jesus ran deeper than that. For the early Christian community who expected the timely return of Jesus in their lifetimes, a more compelling understanding of the crucifixion was needed to deal with the obvious fact that Jesus was not coming back any time soon. It is the compelling notion of theologian B. Hudson McLean that Paul's original understanding of the death of Jesus (that saw the death of Jesus, in the words of New Testament scholar J. Denny Weaver, as "the inauguration of a new age"[20]) did not include the atonement for sin that his later theology did include. McLean suggests that in order to make sense of the absence of Jesus' return, Paul may have appropriated the language of the sacrificial scapegoat that was present throughout the Mediterranean world at that time.[21] The substitutionary role of a scapegoat for the salvation of a community was commonly known and understood throughout the Hellenistic world.

If we assume that Paul engaged in an appropriation (and in modification) of the language and process of contemporary, readily available expulsion rituals to explain the importance of Jesus—even if Jesus was not returning as expected—the substitutionary role of the scapegoat may be viewed as a way of Paul attempting to talk about the viability of belief in Jesus to an increasingly skeptical (and in some cases confused and disappointed) people. This was a brilliant move on Paul's part to make the message of Christianity, the death of Jesus and the promised return of Jesus, meaningful in the face of possible religious collapse. Paul provided a compelling and powerful way of thinking about the meaning of Jesus' life and death that took seriously the dominant mythic structures and language of his day. By critically correlating[22] the expulsion rituals of the Mediterranean region with the knowledge of the life, works, death, and expected hope of the return of Jesus, Paul engaged in a form of theological reflection that took the extant culture seriously.[23]

By appropriating, however critically and constructively, the scapegoat ritual data available from his cultural context, Paul took on at the same time inherent (implicit and explicit) patterns of violence and of the resolution of violence that are problematic in our world today.[24] René Girard, recent Professor of French Language, Literature, and Civilization at Stanford University, has explored the process of scapegoating for more than thirty years.[25] Girard contends that all religious ritual arises from the need to deal with the pervasive problem of violence in society. Human beings have an inherent flaw, the desire to imitate the desire of another person. How is this desire to imitate the desire of the other person (which Girard calls *mimesis*) a flaw?[26] All desire is mediated by a rival. Toril Moi has summarized the triangular flaw by stating, "The subject can only desire an object insofar as another subject already desires the same object. All desire is an imitation of the rival's desire and therefore mimetic."[27] Or in other words, desire attracts desire.[28] The violence that follows to eliminate the rival cannot be stopped—there is no natural braking mechanism for violence born of such envious imitation.

For Girard, the only thing that can stop the violence initiated by mimesis is a ritual killing of a scapegoat. By redirecting the aggression and violence of the parties involved onto a sacrifice, peace is restored, at least temporarily. In the words of Girard,

> Religion instructs men as to what they must and must not do to prevent a recurrence of destructive violence...The surrogate victim alone can save them.[29]

How is a victim, a scapegoat, determined? The choice of a victim (which may be an individual or a whole community or nation of persons, such as the Jews or the Muslims) may be random or may be based on stereotypical fear. Physical appearance and/ or abnormality, behavioral difference (such as gay/lesbian/ bisexual/transsexual persons) social (racial/ethnic, economic, religious) difference, patterns of communal life, attitude toward the government, perceived weakness (women, children, the disabled, old persons), or perceived strength (wealth, size, or power) may give rise to the violent crowd's primarily unconscious transfer of the "original" violence onto a scapegoat.[30] Girard concludes that

> In order for all the persecutors to be inspired by the same faith in the evil power of their victim, the latter must successfully polarize all the suspicions, tensions, and reprisals that poisoned those relationships. The community must effectively be emptied of its poisons. It must feel liberated and reconciled within itself.[31]

This powerful mythic pattern of violence resolution is a compelling way of understanding the purpose and function of all ritual sacrifice in religions, including Christianity. While the remembering or reenactment of the original process of violence and execution of the scapegoat, often performed by groups or "gangs" of people, may be stylized over time (thus removing worshipers from the horror of the origins of the original sacrifice), the ritual sacrifice of the scapegoat continues to give focus and unity to the worshiping community over time. While the memory of the original violence may become buried in the unconscious memory of the worshiping community, and while the liturgical killing of the scapegoat may take on a sanitized or even aesthetically beautiful expression, the execution of the scapegoat lies at the origin of the "holy" practices. In other words, abstraction can distance the worshiping community from the horror of its own violent past, but abstraction cannot remove the fact of violence itself.

The connection that Christianity has with this scapegoat ritual pattern is not lost on Girard, a Roman Catholic. The difference between other world religions and Christianity in this regard, however, focuses on the end of mimetic violence by the Holy Spirit. Girard claims that God "is not dependent on the victimage mechanism."[32] The passion of Jesus, Girard insists, destroyed the unconscious process of victimization, thus exposing the execution of Jesus for what it was, murder. The mythic scapegoat ritual works only when it operates on an unconscious level. When consciousness of the event arose, the death of Jesus no longer served the purposes of the violent gang. The violence and superstition of the scapegoat mythic ritual were exposed for what they were, unacceptable violence that solved nothing at all.[33] Girard concludes:

> By maintaining the word of the Father against violence until the end and by dying for it, Jesus has crossed the abyss separating mankind from the Father. He himself becomes their Paraclete, their protector, and he sends them another Paraclete who will not cease to work in the world to bring forth the truth into the light.[34]

Knowledge of the social injustice of gang violence comes into being at the cross of Christ.[35] Jesus is not a scapegoat sacrificed for the salvation of human beings. Jesus is the incarnate crucified one who suffered and was executed unjustly. The scapegoat myth can be maintained only by terror and violence. The good news is that such myth is exposed as false. In the words of Girard,

> Christian faith consists in this: to think and believe that the resurrection of Christ owes nothing to human violence, by contrast to mythic resurrections, which really stem from collective murders. The resurrection of Christ comes about after his death, inevitably but not immediately; it happens only on the third day, and if we look through a Christian lens, it has its origin in God himself.[36]

The insightful work of Girard helps us begin to understand the extraordinary power of unconscious myth in relation to communal formation and maintenance based on violence, and how Christianity may provide a means of understanding how such formation and maintenance are folly. At the same time, Girard presumes that the negation of mythic violence necessitated the sacrifice of Jesus to expose the insanity of violence—that the genre of sacrificial myth concludes with the narrative of the death of Jesus.

While Girard raises the possibility of the limits of the scapegoat ritual structure and process (a crisis of social disorder arises; guilt and shame are projected onto a scapegoat, who very often embodies signs of a victim; punishment is carried out by death of the victim [or banishment from society]; and the victim is returned in sacred form to reconcile the violence of the community) to put an end to violence, there are significant theological questions that Girard does not address.

First, and perhaps most important for our discussion of violence, is whether mimesis is an adequate starting point for understanding the origin of violence. Are imitation and the ensuing need to eliminate the rival really the basis of human violence? Or are the desire to be in relation with the other person and the fear of being alone the origin of violence? The answer to this question lies in the understanding of what it means to be human. I would contend that it is not mimesis, not rivalry, not competition that is at the root of violence, but the fear of being alone—of being incomplete. Apart from fear, one is in relation with others as a source of joy and fulfillment. In fear, one is in relationship with others only to feel out of control, different, and awkward. In fear, there cannot be a sense of self within diversity, only a sense of self within univocal unity. There is no alternative in fear than to control the chaos of diversity by absorbing or eliminating the other person. It is the rejection of diversity and the compelling need to create all things in one's own image—a process that does not differentiate, but that unifies, absorbs, and destroys the other person or group— that are the ground of violence. With relational violence comes inevitably the growing sense that things cannot and will not change for the better. For the more one tries to be in relation through violence, the more powerful the realization of decadence, that one is losing control of oneself, that things will simply get worse and worse with no possibility of salvation in sight. W. R. Johnson writes of decadence, the sense that life is in decline:

What, then, is decline? What is decadence? It is change, change seen from the advantage point of fear, of fear craving power over what seems to threaten the one who fears.[37]

Diversity gives rise to change, just as uniformity diminishes change. Fear errs on the side of uniformity.

The mythic structure that Girard defines in such a compelling manner requires a scapegoat, not because of mimesis—but because of the fear of being alone and ambivalence about the meaning of self within the context of others who are not like the self. I concur that group violence gives rise across cultures to the religious practice of scapegoating. But unlike Girard, I find the origin of that violence located in a fear of diversity and therefore, a fear of loneliness and a fear of loss of control/loss of self.

What if we did not begin with the assumption of humankind's basic sinfulness but began with the assumption of humankind's basic goodness, of humankind's desire to be in relation with God, self, and others? In a recent address, Archbishop Desmond Tutu reflected:

Yes, wonderfully, exhilaratingly, we have this extraordinary capacity for good. Fundamentally, we are good; we are made for love, for compassion, for caring, for sharing, for peace and reconciliation, for transcendence, for the beautiful, for the true and the good.[38]

Certainly Tutu is not suggesting that human beings cannot demonstrate a vast capacity for violence, as evidenced in his own South Africa. But to be created in the image of God means first and foremost to be created for the love, compassion, caring, and sharing that Tutu affirms. Said another way, human beings are created for doxology. Human beings are created to live in creative and life-giving interdependence. Human beings are created to take pleasure in all creation.[39] Self-sufficiency and pride that arise from discovery of self in life-giving relation with others is not the result of rivalry, but of love.[40]

I have no doubt that the desire of unhealthy imitation that Girard describes exists among persons in the world. But I do doubt that this desire is the origin of all violence.[41] The desire to be in relation with others may be misdirected and twisted. The origin of violence is the desire to be in relation with God and with others—but in ways that veer from God's image. A subsequent expression of misdirected relationality may well be inappropriate imitation and envy of the other person. But this is not the origin of violence, only one expression of its practice.

While Girard does not propose that God expected Jesus to be the obedient child who would take away the sins of the world through sacrificial death, Girard's proposal leaves us rather uncertain about God's role in the execution of Jesus. If viewed from a Christian perspective, we are left with a pivotal question. Was the death of Jesus necessary to expose the folly of violence and of the scapegoat myth? Girard's thesis would seem to say yes, that the death of Jesus was unique to the process of revealing the efficacy of the scapegoat as a lie.

The question of the execution of Jesus cannot be cast in functional terms: What was accomplished by the death of Jesus? The question of the murder of Jesus is an interpersonal (relational) one: Who among us is being executed and humiliated today? It is true that the death of Jesus exposed violence as absurdity. This is not the same thing as suggesting that the death of Jesus, by exposing the folly of violence, destroyed a scapegoat myth. The death of any human being created in the image of God exposes the scapegoat myth to be false. That Christians may have a special resource in the execution of Jesus for remembering the futility of violence is not questioned. But to suggest that the death of Jesus is somehow unique in its ability to unmask violence, however, is false.

In Paul the scapegoat myth continues to be an underlying frame of interpretation for the gospel and Christian life—and this is an unresolved problem for Christian corporate understanding and self-understanding today. Indeed, what is clear from this discussion of violence thus far is that God did not will Jesus to sacrifice his life and his dignity in order to forgive human sin. Human violence is an expression of spiritual crisis, when relations with God, with others, with self, and with the earth become misdirected through choice or through inheritance. Love does not require the sacrifice of self, but the discovery of self in life-giving relations.[42]

By reinterpreting the sacrificial scapegoat myth and imposing it on his understanding of the meaning of the life and death of Jesus, Paul was able to communicate his understanding of the gospel to his culture and his times. If it is true that artists are only rarely conscious of the meaning of the works of art that they create, it is even likely that Paul did not understand the deep significances of the narrative framework he used to describe the meaning of the life and death of Jesus. While the mythic scapegoat narrative structure may have helped Paul expose the folly of violence, Paul did not stop there. In a very real sense, Paul has perpetuated the values of the scapegoat myth (selfless, sacrificial, and helpless acceptance of violence as God wills it for the good of the whole) as something to be imitated in faithful Christian life. Paul did not realize fully that unjust suffering serves no purpose of God. He did realize that the resurrection of Jesus signaled a new age. Both views are in the Pauline writings, existing side by side.[43] Theologian Marjorie Suchocki has written that "to sin against the other is to violate the other; to be sinned against is to be violated."[44] Using the language of Suchocki, God did not sin against Jesus, any more than God sins against humankind.[45]

God is not saving us from lives of violence by means of violence, suffering, abuse, or humiliation. Rita Nakashima Brock writes, "violence fragments the self, creating selflessness, and it destroys love."[46] Violence, suffering, abuse, and humiliation reveal the futility of these attempts to be in relation with ourselves, with others, and with God. God is saving us through God's continued faithful love through the community of faith that is empowered by the Holy Spirit. In the words of theologian Delores Williams, we are "redeemed though Jesus' *ministerial* vision of life and not through his death."[47] Salvation, then, is the continuing work of the Holy Spirit through the church and often beyond the limits of the church. The Spirit is bound by no single religious form, but blows where it desires.

Where Is God in Violent Situations?

Let us assume that for Christians, the execution of Jesus helps us see more clearly the folly of violence. The question, "Where was God when Jesus was murdered?" continues to be problematic— even if, as Girard contends, God did not require human sacrifice in order to be appeased. Because God did not intervene by saving Jesus from the cross, cannot God be understood as "a child abuser or a bystander to violence against his own child"?[48]

In Elie Wiesel's book *Night*, a book that describes the horror of a young boy's experiences in a Nazi death camp, a well-known passage describes the horror of the murder of a child. Torture and murder were commonplace in these camps. In one instance, three persons were to be hanged in front of the prisoners. Wiesel tells us of three nooses that were placed around the necks of three persons—two adults and a child—with satanic efficiency. Suddenly, from the group of prisoners forced to watch this execution, the words rang out, "Where is God? Where is He?" As the three persons were hanged, the prisoners were required to march past, apparently as a means of intimidation. Wiesel describes the dreadful scene. While the adults died almost immediately, the child, whose weight was not great enough to allow the rope to do its work efficiently, was brutalized:

> For more than half an hour he stayed there, struggling between life and death, dying in slow agony under our eyes. And we had to look him full in the face. He was still alive when I passed in front of him. His tongue was still red, his eyes not yet glazed.
>
> Behind me, I heard the same man asking: "Where is God now?" And I heard a voice within me answer him: "Where is He? Here He is—He is hanging here on this gallows...."
>
> That night the soup tasted of corpses.[49]

At first glance, the very idea that God was hanging on the gallows seems shocking, repulsive, and perhaps even offensive. For some, this assertion that God is hanging on the gallows in the form of a young boy is nothing more than an immature and irrational response to the horror of such a scene. Certainly, one could argue, God is infinite and cannot be confined in the body of a single Jewish child. Certainly, one could argue, God could not die by strangulation at the hands of a murderer.

Yet this is the case. The story from Wiesel's own experiences in the death camp is a story of God's presence and of God's absence. In the moment of God's absence, God is present. God's absence is real. It is not a situation in which it merely feels or seems that God is absent. God is actually and fully absent, while at the same moment God is actually and fully present. Holding two statements to be truthful that do not appear to be logically related is known as a paradox. Pastoral theologian Seward Hiltner once observed:

> A paradox, we may remind ourselves, is not necessarily a contradiction. It does represent our belief in our commitment to at least two statements of truth or value despite the fact that there is some logical contradiction between them. Some paradoxes turn out to be merely problems that can be solved by discovery of some principle demonstrating that the logical contradiction was only apparent and not permanent. The genuine paradox,

however, persists in all its contradictoriness even when study casts light on any or all of its elements.[50]

Wherever people suffer unjustly, God's presence is intense. The quality of the intensity of presence is absence. Said another way, God's presence requires absence. This is genuine paradox, the kind of paradox that God reveals to us through incarnation.

The presence of God in our lives and in the world is an experience of God's absence. God is not merely present in absence. God's absence *is* God's presence, and God's presence *is* God's absence. To know God intimately is dangerous to our inherently human need to define God in comforting and manageable ways.

Absence is the promise of the unambiguous fidelity of God. God's fidelity is an experience of the terror of the fullness of absence and the fullness of presence in the selfsame moment.[51] The "moment" of God's absence is beyond time and touches at the abyss and height and width of all eternity.

Apart from this unresolved and irresolvable paradox of God's presence and God's absence, theological reflection cannot take place. Apart from this paradox, theological reflection is a dangerous mocking of God. Such theological reflection is dangerous because it is false in its understanding of the paradoxical nature of God. Where is God to be found? God is to be found where most fully absent: among the victims of poverty, oppression, violence, and hatred. In these contexts it is discovered that God is absent, and this absence alone is the presence of God.

The unresolved tension between God's presence and God's absence, that is, the context or "playground" of theological reflection and praxis, is existentially dislocating and uncomfortable. In many educational teaching methods, creative activities hope for an "A-Ha!" moment in which contradictions are collapsed, and psychic tension released. While there may be a moment of insight related to the relation of God's simultaneous presence and absence by an individual or a group, instead of resolving the inherent paradox, the "A-Ha!" deepens the awareness of God's absence and presence—*deepening rather than resolving the mystery of the paradox, as well as the felt discomfort of deepened psychic tension.*

Conversion, rather than being a state of the resolution of paradox, is the ongoing recognition that theological reflection and praxis take place only within the context of the "force field" created by the unresolved tension of God's absence. God's absence and God's presence are not dialectical (that is, resolving in a new synthesis), but paradoxical (that is, without resolution or new synthesis). Conversion, turning from sin, invites persons into the mystery of paradox.

The words of Jesus as given form in Mark 15 point to the depths of agony this deepening sense of God's absence and presence bring to those who open themselves to the paradoxical mystery of God's incarnation:

> When it was noon, darkness came over the whole land until three in the afternoon. At three o'clock, Jesus cried out with a loud voice, "Eloi, Eloi, lema sabachthani?" which means, "My God, my God, why have you forsaken me?" (Mk. 15:33–34)

It would appear that even Jesus did not fully understand the depths of God's presence until God's absence weighed upon him. In a very real sense, Jesus realized his full humanity only as his sense of God's absence allowed God to become fully present—fully no-thing. The question of Jesus, not unlike the question overheard by the young Wiesel is the central question of all true faith, including Christian faith. The question is not one of accusation nor of blaming, but one of relation. "Where are you, God?" is a question that many of us have asked. The silent response of God is simple, but paradoxical—"Here I am."[52]

In the moment of agony on the cross, the moment in which Jesus learned what it meant to be fully human by understanding God's absence as God's presence, those who stood around the cross denied this revelatory moment. It was too bizarre to believe. Reinterpretation of the words of Jesus into a more comforting and familiar frame of reality was the way those who observed the dying Jesus chose to deal with the gospel of absence. "Listen, he is calling for Elijah" (Mk. 15:35) was not the result of a mumbling Jesus, his words too difficult to understand because of the pain and trauma of crucifixion. This response was not the result of too much noisy confusion at the cross. This response was the response of the rejection of the God revealed in Jesus, a rejection of the gospel. Rather than dealing with the terror of God's presence/absence in violence, a comforting retreat was made, "Listen, he is calling for Elijah." This was a self-protecting statement of domestication and denial of God's presence in the *absence*. To speak of the absence of God is no less ignored by people today. Dorothee Soelle has written:

> Contemporary civil religion—the kind that equates Christianity with the capitalist system—needs neither an inward journey nor a return journey; neither does it

experience danger. Within such a religion God is a symbol that guarantees order.[53]

To identify with those who suffer unjustly is to open oneself and one's community to the possibility of God's absence where God alone is present. To enter into solidarity with those who suffer is to open oneself to the possibility of God's transforming presence in absence. Pastoral theologian Sharon G. Thornton concludes, "solidarity at a most basic level involves our becoming vulnerable to others who are suffering. It means we become open to being transformed by those with whom we become united in resistance and struggle for wholeness."[54] There is a direct relation between the human body and knowing God. Jesus suffered on the cross with all the pain and agony of any person who has been tortured. The suffering of Jesus was not merely a symbolic literary device. The suffering of Jesus was carnal.

How do we know God? We know God through our solidarity with the unjustly oppressed. We know God in the terror of absence, a place where total mystery abides. That total mystery is called love. This love takes such historical forms as justice, righteousness, and the protection of the outcast.[55] Participation with this pattern of love is more than an exercise of detached charity. It demands taking on the pain of the other as one's own. It demands passive acceptance of the possibility of non-being. It demands selflessness, an attitude and action of heart, so that God may love.

Nothing is intrinsically "saintly" or "sinful" about suffering. Romanticizing victimization or suffering is completely non-Christian. All persons are called to "cooperate with God."[56] Those in comfort go to those who suffer because there is suffering, not in order to guarantee some special favor of God through possible martyrdom.[57]

The power of God may be understood only if one discusses powerlessness. In powerlessness, God is strong. In solidarity with those who suffer unjustly, God is abandoning God's own yearning to live, give life, and create. This strong but powerless God is a God in mission, one who calls the church to become a part of this mission. When a starving child in the Sudan dies, God is not merely present as some visitor who comes to pay last respects. God becomes incarnate in that child, and that child dies for the sin of all humankind. Every time death comes at the hand of the oppressor, God cries out, "Forgive them; for they do not know what they are doing!" (Lk. 23:34). Every time death comes at the hand of the oppressor, God dies—only to be reborn again in the agony of the pain of those who face death for the human evil of the world. Again, this does not imply salvation through suffering. Nothing is intrinsically salvific about suffering. It does recognize the fact of the permanent agony and suffering of God where injustice dehumanizes the individual.

It seems overwhelming, this solidarity of God with the oppressed. In the United States, that symbol of global affluence and gluttony, some 100,000 children are homeless every night. Every day some 8,000 children are added to the list of those reported abused or neglected. Each day some 30 children die because of poverty.[58] This is within a context of affluence, where 80 percent of the earth's resources are consumed by 20 percent of the earth's population. These children are the dwelling places of God. These are the voices of God calling the peoples of the world to repentance. These little voices join with oppressed children, as well as their mothers, all over the globe. Their voices together are deafening, only to be ignored or silenced by the oppressing privilege of a few.[59] God is not silent in our day. God is crying out with a million different voices, in a million different dialects and languages, in a million different regions of the world. The world is full of God's cries of agony, pain, and hurt.

Why do we not hear God's voice among us? Because we listen for God's word in places where God does not dwell. God does not dwell in a safe place. God does not dwell in a sanctuary. God does not dwell in places of plenty and security. God dwells in those who suffer unjust violence by the hands and words of another. God dwells in the pain of mental anguish. God dwells among the poor and oppressed. "Here He is—He is hanging here on this gallows."[60] This voice of God is not a cheap romanticizing of the poor and oppressed. This voice of God, rather, decries the injustices that negates voice. Reflecting on the book of Lamentations, biblical scholar Kathleen O'Connor comes dangerously close to this conclusion. Curiously, we may recall, the voice of God at first glance is absent in this biblical book of exile. She writes:

> The biblical book of Lamentations refuses denial, practices truth-telling, and reverses amnesia. It invites the readers into pain, chaos, and brutality, both human and divine. It conveys effects of trauma, loss, and grief beyond tears. Because God's voice is absent, it gives primacy to suffering voices like no other biblical book.[61]

But is God's voice absent from the suffering voices? In the paradox of God's absent voice, the voice of God cries out itself in "suffering voices like no other book."[62]

It is God who seeks to rupture dominant ideologies that survive on the suffering of the oppressed. It is God who initiates this social challenge, and it is God who invites us to work in partnership for a renewed earth. The troublesome biblical story of the early life of Jesus, as recorded in Matthew 2:13ff. is sobering in this context. Disfigured by the fear of loss of control, Herod sought to cleanse the earth of all perceived threat, and the tears of mothers (the tears of God) could protest, but not stop, the egocentric madness. It may be concluded that fleeing political violence is sometimes all that can be done and that God is incapable of stopping the slaughter of children in Rama, let alone of children of Taliban members, Iraqi children, impoverished children in the United States, or children of Angola. I assert that hearing the voice of God in the cries of children around the world is, in the words of Rita Nakashima Brock, the basis for "empowered people to affirm their own agency, to resist abuse, to take responsibility for ethical discernment, and to work for justice."[63] It is the life of Jesus and his resurrection in the life of the community of faith that bring the hope of salvation from violence into the world—not his execution.

This self-limitation of God, to incarnate God's self in the pain and suffering of the unjustly oppressed, may seem upsetting to many Christians at first. For many Christians, the poor and oppressed are to be served, and God's presence is to be found in the server's altruistic actions. This is incorrect. Christians serve the poor and oppressed because this is where they may meet the incarnate God face-to-face. Christians serve the poor and oppressed because through participation in the powerlessness and absence of God in the face of suffering, they come to know the presence and power of God. God is not revealed in the actions of compassion of the Christian on behalf of the suffering. God is revealing God's self in the suffering itself. God is crying out, "Stop this madness! If you seek me, if you desire to know me, work for peace with justice!" And what if the violence leads to silence, and the person is unable to cry out in pain? Then we become the advocate, the voice of God's agony on that person's behalf. It is irresponsible in our times to encourage those who seek to be faithful Christians in the world, especially those who are without power, to be self-sacrificial and quiet. To imagine that Jesus was being obedient to (Father) God through self-sacrifice is a misinterpretation of the gospel. This is not an appropriate pattern of life and of death to emulate. Violence cannot be transformed by means of this understanding of Jesus.[64]

If to listen for the word of God is to bring us into the presence of the suffering of human beings, God will be found in rather unlikely places. Unjust violence and oppression know no physical or political boundaries, no religious tradition, no gender or racial or ethnic identity. God loves the world. In that love, God chooses to risk everything in the process of solidarity with those in pain. God is God of the whole world. God is not Jewish, Christian, Hindu, Buddhist, nor Muslim. God is God. Christians serve all brothers and sisters without regard to religious or national identity because they realize that God is present wherever people suffer unjustly. Christians participate in God's work in the world when they listen for God's word as revealed in those who suffer. The good news is that Christians affirm God's presence in absence, God's power in powerlessness, by attending to the pain and suffering of others.

Listening for God's Word in a Violent World

Listening for God's word in God's absence is related closely to the concept of hospitality. Classicist Susan Ford Wiltshire has written that, "modern hospitality is typically a transaction among friends. Ancient hospitality was a transaction among strangers. Modern hospitality reinforces our familiarities. Ancient hospitality alters us by exposing us to outsiders. Ancient hospitality—*xenia* in the Greek tradition and *hospitium* or *ius hospitii* in the Roman— thus provides a meeting place for the public and private realms."[65]

The process or method of knowing God that takes seriously the absence of God in solidarity with the oppressed is hospitality in that ancient sense. While there are those occasions within the life of the church that call for mutual caregiving, the missional attitude of solidarity opens individuals and groups to the unpredictability of influence and change (conversion) that comes with the risk of identifying with those outside the community. It is important to see that in this perspective, knowing God is fundamentally an act of relational risk, one that presumes that knowledge of God comes primarily from outside the Christian community. This understanding of God's word for the Christian community is foreign to most denominational groups, which tend to be introverted by internal analysis of experience and texts rather than propelled in an extroverted manner by the texts into the world beyond the community. Mission is not only a "going out" with the gospel into the world but also a "discovery of" the gospel in the world.

Such an understanding of communal identity and formation is an affirmation of the importance of pluralism and diversity for the ongoing vital life of the Christian community. M. M. Bakhtin once wrote:

In the historical period of ancient Greek life—a period that was, linguistically speaking, stable and monoglotic—all plots, all subject and thematic material, the entire basic stock of images, expressions and intonations, arose from within the very heart of the native language. Everything that entered from the outside (and that was a great deal) was assimilated in a powerful and confident environment of closed-off monoglossia, one that viewed the polyglossia of the barbarian world with contempt.[66]

Christianity is fundamentally a pluralistic (polyglotic) religious tradition, though in most of its social and political manifestations it has appeared to reflect monoglotic national or xenophobic interests. Hospitality calls the Christian community to listen for the word of God wherever that word arises, including in the stranger. In fact, knowing God is linked directly to conversation with the stranger.

A fascinating thing happens to the Christian as she or he attends to God's word in the stranger. In solidarity with the stranger, the Christian becomes a risk to the community's status quo and becomes a place of God's absence and God's presence.

To share in the suffering of others is an act of hospitality in which one hears the word of God in the other, and the word of God (miraculously!) becomes enfleshed in the hospitality-giver as well. "You" become a presence in the absence that is the presence of God. Having once experienced the absent presence of God, one is marked permanently. Another word for *mark* is *character*. One's character is marked by God's absence.

In those moments of silence and emptiness filled by the Spirit, we are seized with terror. We are drawn to see the fragmentation of our lives without the mask of civility and order. To be Christian is to be radically pluralistic, radically polyglotic. God's presence permeates the whole world. Catherine LaCugna has put it this way:

God's glory is especially manifested in "the little ones," those broken by pain and rejection, those considered unattractive and undesirable, the lepers, defined differently in each society, the public sinners, the ritually impure. All the "inglorious" ones are to be sought out if we wish to behold the glory of God. Jesus grasped this clearly.[67]

It would be easy to understand such a quotation in a violent and inappropriate way. For years, wealthy churches in the United States have had what might be called "field trips" to less affluent countries. Locations of poverty and physical need are referred to often as "mission projects," and the desire to help the less fortunate is often genuine and heartfelt. There is nothing inherently wrong with sharing resources with our brothers and sisters throughout the world. But when such good intention becomes an act of "helping" rather than hearing God's word through solidarity with those who suffer, a colonialist pattern of altruistic dependency may easily displace love.

Author Toni Morrison has written about the problems inherent in the relation between those with power and those without power in her book *Playing in the Dark: Whiteness and the Literary Imagination*.[68] For Morrison, looking at a person as an object is an abusing act of power in which the person looked at is intentionally silenced.[69] This sort of *looking* is an example of *force*. It is difficult for many of us to think that our well-intentioned acts of charity to those who are suffering could be acts of dehumanization and violence. If a person is starving, does it make any difference whether the food is given in an act of *looking* or in an act of loving solidarity? Sharing food *as if* it is an act of hospitality is an act of violence by those who would seek to dehumanize the hungry person. Giving food as an act of self-assured charity to the object is an act of violence by those who would seek to dehumanize the hungry person. Feeding the hungry as an act of violence turns the human being into a thing. It is a form of force that ultimately kills the human spirit.

Once again let us turn to Elie Wiesel's *Night* for an example of false charity, dehumanization, looking, and giving food to the hungry. A train containing Jews who had been without food for many days was crossing Germany. The train stopped at a German township.

> A crowd of workmen and curious spectators had collected along the train. They had probably never seen a train with such a cargo. Soon, nearly everywhere, pieces of bread were being dropped into the wagons. The audience stared at these skeletons of men, fighting one another to the death for a mouthful.[70]

There was no hospitality by the workmen, only staring from a vantage point of power. Looking took on the form of violence as the bread was cast to persons (seen by the workmen as animals) who were starving unjustly. This was not solidarity, but raw barbarity. Bread at what cost? Bread at the cost of dignity, love, and human being.

Did the German workmen realize that God was embodied in each of those Jewish men who were starving? No, they did not get close enough to hear God's word. What would they have heard if they had listened? I do not know. But I am guessing that they may have heard something like, "Stop this insanity! I am your brother! God created me with the breath of life! Stop this insanity before it is too late!" According to Wiesel's account, no one tried to stop the train. No one protested. Certainly, God could not speak through a starving Jew. And so, the German workmen stared and threw scraps of bread.

Psychologist Robert Coles tells the story of a little girl named Ruby Bridges. Ruby was an African American child who lived in New Orleans during desegregation of schools. Only six years old, Ruby would go through mobs of angry white people every day on her way to school. Police escorts could not stop the foul words, spitting, and attempted acts of physical violence. Ruby would stop in front of the mob three times every day; her lips would move as the federal marshals ushered her into and out of the public school. Coles discovered in conversations with Ruby that she was praying for those who sought her destruction. Coles asked:

> "Do you pray for them a lot, Ruby?" And then I made the point that this was after all, three times a day. Then with her silence, I decided to take a new tack. I said, "Ruby, what do you say in this prayer?"
>
> She said, "I always say the same thing."
>
> (At which point I am sure the old psychologist, if he had electrodes connected to me, would have noticed dilation of the pupils, slight increase in the blood pressure.) I said, "What's that?"
>
> She said, "I say, 'Please, God, try to forgive them, those people, because they don't know what they are doing.'"[71]

Listening for the word of God is the opposite of looking or staring. In God's absence, God became fully present not only in the words of Ruby, but to Ruby herself. Her act of self-assertive faith and compassionate justice, remembering and forgiving, represented theological reflection and action at their most mature, at their deepest depths. How totally unexpected this great theologian of the Christian faith must have appeared then. How unexpected are our reflections about her now. In the words of Thomas Aquinas, "Age of body does not determine age of soul."[72]

Ruby helps us understand hospitality now. She leads us to a new awareness of God's culture that we are able to deny only at our present peril. Once God has revealed Godself, it is impossible to contain the revelation. Ruby was a leader and a teacher. She helped others see God's culture more clearly. To identify with her, to act in solidarity with Ruby, does not come from a motivational technique. It comes as a gift from God to respond to God in faith and love to the vision ushered in "by the least of these."

In traditional Trinitarian language, the "power" of the Holy Spirit is the gift from God's saving love in Jesus Christ that inspires persons to act in ways that are congruent with the gospel. From what does God save us? God saves us, through the power of the Holy Spirit, from violence in our personal and communal lives.

The risk of faith is given form and direction by hospitality. Hospitality invites voices from outside the community of origin into the community. Hospitality listens attentively to the voices of the oppressed because that is where the absent God is speaking in God's presence. Hospitality is fundamentally pluralistic and attends to the incarnation of God wherever God chooses to speak.

Summary

We have traveled together a very long way in a very short time! Remember that the primary purpose of reading a book is to be in conversation with its author. Some of you have many questions you would like to ask of me! This is exactly as it should be and indicates you have taken seriously the argument of this first chapter. God desires us to be in relation and draws us to Godself our whole lives. This yearning to be in relation with God, and therefore with other persons, is part of what it means to be created in the image of God. As Christians, we desire to have our lives be more and more in tune with the God whom we adore and worship. Discerning between doxology and sin, then, becomes a practical matter of positive living.

As we reflect more and more about doxology and sin, our thoughts turn more intentionally to the meaning of the life and death of Jesus. The meaning of the life and death of Jesus was best articulated in the Bible by Paul.[73] But we know through our discussion of Bronfenbrenner that all of us live our lives in social contexts (which contain their own ideas and stories) that shape who we are, how we communicate with others, and how we understand ourselves in relation with others. Scholars help us understand one of the dominant ways people understood victimization and violence present in the Mediterranean world during the time of Paul—the scapegoating myth. René Girard is particularly helpful in exploring the details of such a myth. I conclude that by looking at the work of a person such as Girard, we come to understand the importance of thinking about God in ways that are nonviolent, that are relational, and that are empowering.

We are moving ever deeper into the mystery of our faith when we begin to wonder about the ways in which God speaks to us today, in the midst of a violent world. Some of us probably thought about the world as a violent place only abstractly until September 11. But most of us today wonder aloud where God is speaking God's word today, in a world especially broken by unnecessary violence. By reflecting on the possibility of paradox when thinking about God, we conclude that hospitality is a primary way to open ourselves to God—where we least expect it.

We now turn to a case study of a young boy who was caught in the web of one form of violence that is very much around us in our neighborhoods, our states, our countries, and our world today. As we discuss bullying as a public example of violence, the foundations laid by this chapter will help us begin to interpret this contemporary crisis of relating to others. We shall discover that bullying is fundamentally an outward sign of spiritual crisis.

CHAPTER 2

Karl's Fall to Violence

A Case Study

Let us bring what we now know in general about violence and
Christian faith to the careful consideration of a specific case study
about violence. In the years following the 1983 Norwegian Ministry
of Education's nationwide anti-bullying campaign (a creative
response to the deaths of two child suicides that were attributed to
bullying), there has been a global renewed interest in child-on-child
violence. But I find that virtually no research exists about the long-
term effects of childhood bullying for Christian persons. Over the
past seven years, I have been talking with Christian adults about
their memories of childhood violence. At first persons came to talk
with me as the result of an ad I ran in my seminary's weekly
newspaper. Over time, however, persons have chosen to talk with
me about their experiences of childhood bullying because of "word
of mouth." I have talked with men and women from all over the
United States, with Anglo Americans, African Americans, and
Asian Americans. They ranged in age from twenty-five to sixty-
eight. Some of the persons I interviewed were bullies. Some were
bullied. Some were both bullied and bullies. The case that follows

31

stands out for its honesty, its insight, and the courage of its storyteller, Karl. This case embodies the dominant trends and themes that came up again and again during my interviews.

When I asked Karl about the possibility of permission to use his story as a case study in this book, he responded positively, generously, and graciously. Karl's courage to share his story was genuine, remarkable, and moving. Why would Karl want to share his story of childhood violence with us? The answer is simple. Karl is a man who yearns to help others put a stop to child-on-child violence. In a very real way, Karl is choosing to act as a child advocate on behalf of those children caught in the web of violence.

This case is not intended to be normative for all cultural and/ or gender situations. It would be both inappropriate and impossible to generalize this case beyond its own contexts. At the same time, the dominant themes raised by this case (or by issues you see that are not raised by this case) provide an opportunity for discussion about violence in childhood, and the implications of that violence for religious self-understanding. The discussion that you have about the case is as important, if not more important, than the specific case itself. There is much the case tells us, and much the case leaves unclear. How we interpret the case is as important as the information that the case provides, because the way we interpret the case says something important about the ways we view violence and about violence in our soiciety and our world.

"Karl" is a pseudonym. Specific locations and other names have been changed. This will not be an easy case for many persons to read. It is one thing to talk about violence in the abstract (a valuable and important way to gain understanding, for sure), but it is quite another to hear another person's concrete experience with violence. It is not necessary to rush through this case to get to the next chapter. Read this chapter at a pace that is appropriate and comfortable for you. Reflect often on the content of this case study, and with the understanding of violence presented in the previous chapter. Wonder about the times you have been a bully. Wonder about the times you have been bullied. All adults have been bullied, and all adults have been the bully. None of us is exempt from the importance of the issues raised by Karl's story.

This case study is presented in a way that is primarily descriptive. In chapter 1, we explored one possible Christian approach to understanding the dynamics of violence. In this chapter, a specific example of relational violence is explored. This chapter prepares you for chapter 3, which brings the experience of

Karl back into deliberate conversation with chapter 1. Said another way, experience is important; but experience without critical reflection almost always results in stagnation and fatalism. Experience alone cannot be transformational. Experience that is reflected on has the potential for growth and for transformation. Read the case at least three times before moving on to the analysis section of this chapter.

Case Study

Karl is a white male, aged 42. From the middle of seventh grade to ninth grade, Karl was bullied by three boys: "One thin and wiry, one big and fat, and one small." All three were older than he.

Karl was in Catholic school until the seventh grade and was confirmed there. He had friends. In the middle of seventh grade, he transferred to the public school. His father and his mother were factory workers and apparently could no longer afford private education. It was in his new school that he met the bullies for the first time.

In the parochial school, Karl had worn a blue uniform and black tie. Neither he nor his parents knew what kids wore in public school. His mother bought him Hush Puppies, skin-tight high-water pants, a Navy peacoat, and a black dickey. "I looked like Richie Cunningham from Happy Days! It was quite a transformation from the angelic altar boy I once was in the Catholic school. I was new, alone, and vulnerable," Karl lamented. "The sharks in the public school knew it, too."

While the physical assaults against Karl were irregular, his fear was constant. Every day in class, a boy from the group of bullies would taunt Karl by threatening, "After school tonight!" Karl would try to go home "by stealth." He would borrow someone's sweater or wear a friend's hat to camouflage himself, or deliberately walk home with girls. He would take several Alka Seltzer tablets with warm water and saltines to "fake throwing up" within the hearing range of his mother so that he did not have to go to school. This happened daily for two entire school years. Karl feared his tormenters. He was afraid to go to dances, department stores, or sporting events alone, and he was too embarrassed about his cowardice to confide in either parent about the bullies. Teachers observed the bullies as they approached and threatened Karl, but did nothing to relieve him of his tormenters.

The abuse Karl endured throughout the seventh and eighth grades was not limited to threats of physical terror. One time during recess, a group of bullies and onlookers formed a circle around him and forced the weakest child in the circle, "the runt," to go into the middle of the circle and fight Karl.[1] Karl knew if he fought the runt, the entire class would turn against him for hitting a weakling. Karl said, "Terror was my everyday experience. I could not imagine my life ever changing."

Karl went from a solid B+ student in his old school to making only D's and F's—barely passing. In a desperate attempt to change his "Howdy Doody" image, Karl began smoking cigarettes, cursing, and shoplifting 45-rpm records from the department stores he once avoided. At thirteen, he tattooed the letter *K* onto his arm with India ink and a safety pin. The principal saw it and reported it to his parents. His father said, "You a**hole, you're going to wash dishes until that god**** thing wears off!" That evening, Karl scrubbed the fresh wound with a Brillo pad while washing dishes. He learned that the tattoo was permanent. To this thirteen-year-old, scrubbing away layers of bleeding, blemished flesh was the only alternative to a lifetime of washing dishes. The site became infected, and the tattoo was removed surgically. Nearly thirty years later, Karl showed me the scar.

In the eighth grade, Karl moved into deep despair and became withdrawn. He had become a laughingstock with the girls, none of whom would come near him. Karl had become the object of ridicule among the seventh- and eighth-graders. Life at home was no better for Karl, who suffered both physically and emotionally at the hands of his alcoholic father. Karl knew of no one he could trust, of no one to whom he could turn for help. He had lost confidence in authority figures: teachers, parents, priests, and the police.

In class one afternoon, he reached "a boiling point." A bully leaned over and whispered in Karl's ear, "After school tonight." Karl reached over his shoulder, grabbed the bully by the hair, and slammed the bully's head into the desk as hard as he could. Having stunned the bully, Karl dragged him across the classroom to a window and repeatedly smashed the bully's face into the glass. Karl admits that these behaviors were "suicidal," but he had stopped caring. He felt little regard for himself, and none for others.

Karl then decided to hunt down each of the bullies—one at a time. "I became totally vicious. I became my own worst nightmare." He was terrified of what he was doing, but also took great pleasure in seeing the other bullies suffer. "I was never a bully," Karl insists. "They were the bullies. Ironic, isn't it? The violence they taught me came back to haunt them." Unable to understand what he had become, Karl started sniffing glue. He smoked openly in front of authority figures, continued shoplifting (and was eventually arrested), attacked classmates for the slightest provocation, and inappropriately touched girls in full view of classmates.

"They graduated me from the eighth grade, but I wasn't prepared," he said. Soon Karl had racked up four arrests—one for beating up his girlfriend's father (girls now found Karl attractive in his violence), and one for beating up his own father. Alcohol abuse, stolen cars, and violence were soon a part of his daily life. On his way out of a dance with a girlfriend, one of her male friends told her good-bye, "just good-bye." Karl put the friend in the hospital—he beat the boy's head and face so hard that he "ripped the gums away from the mouth and his ears away from his head." Karl dropped out of high school in his junior year. By the time he reached his sixteenth birthday, he had eight arrests and five convictions. Although Karl admits no coercion by the judge at his last sentencing hearing, he did see the judge's wisdom in pressing him to choose military service in lieu of a 120–day sentence in the state's correctional center (in addition to two years of adult probation).

As Karl told this story—it was the first time he had told it to anyone—he moved about the room as though he were in a virtual reality system. Arms flew as if he were hitting another person. He took steps as if he were at the dance. Putting into words what was for so long silent was a powerful and moving experience for both Karl and me. When I asked if he had ever prayed for the bullies, I caught a brief but powerful glimpse into the rage of his earlier years. "No! Never! They all robbed me of my education. They forced this thirteen-year-old into a situation that was beyond my control. Five years after beating my first bully I was in a combat zone in Vietnam, guarding a check point, while the bullies and my classmates sashayed their way to the prom," he replied, his hand pounding the arm of his chair. Some thirty years had passed since Karl had first been bullied. But the memories and emotions were immediate and fresh and physically acted out.

Analysis of the Case
Karl: Pre-Public School

Let us begin discussion of this case by returning to those categories of human development proposed by Urie Brofenbrenner: microsystem, mesosystem, exosystem, macrosystem, and chronosystem.

Where did Karl have face-to-face relationships with persons and groups on an ongoing basis? We learn that Karl's microsystem (family, school, peers, church) shifted over time, which means that the microsystem and the chronosystem were very important variables in his self-understanding. Before the seventh grade, Karl went to a private Catholic school. By inference, it appears that Karl was a good student with friends. This was a Catholic family. Karl alludes not only to his sheltered Catholic school experience but to patterns of authority in such a setting, such as priests and teachers. His family was blue-collar, working class. It sounds as if his parents worked very hard, and might have been available to him for only short periods during the day. While Karl does not speak in detail about his father's alcoholism, it no doubt contributed to a pattern of unacceptable anger. It would appear that Karl was not so much loved by his father as intimidated. Certainly, Karl does not describe a loving and reciprocally respectful relation with his father. His mother is a shadowy figure, one who provides clothing (a caring behavior both before and after the seventh grade), but perhaps with not much time or energy for loving.

Where was Karl affirmed and valued in his microsystem (family, school, peers, church) relations? It can be inferred that he had good friends, that he did well in school, and that his self-esteem was linked with both of these. He was Catholic, which gave his life a certain security and predictability. He knew how to act, how to dress, and how to get along in his familiar environment. His family system was under great stress: the alcoholism of the father, the virtual absence of the mother, and indications of financial difficulty make it seem as if Karl was very much alone at home, while his hardworking parents did attempt to provide for his physical needs. There is no indication, explicit nor implicit, that Karl expressed love and trust in his parents, nor that his parents expressed any love and trust to Karl—so important in the development of self-esteem and social competence.[2]

In regard to the mesosystem, the way the various systems of the microsystem (family, school, peers, church) interacted, we encounter ambiguous relationships. While it is possible at a certain level that the values of the home, school, and church were interrelated by the values of Catholicism, it is clear that Karl was regarded more positively in school and with peers than at home. We may infer that there were hierarchical understandings of relationship in the school and at home, but that the relation with the father did not give the same affirmation, say, as being a good student—or being an altar boy.

The exosystem (friends, neighbors, parents' workplace) seems almost irrelevant at a certain level. Neighbors or friends of the family, for example, are strangely absent from Karl's narrative. It almost sounds as if there was home, church, and school—and little else. How much communication actually took place among home, church, and school? It is doubtful that very much conversation on Karl's behalf took place among these three settings. Certainly, the context of "work" had enormous consequence for Karl—in terms of his relationship with his parents as well as his ability to attend a private school. We know that the Vietnam "conflict" was taking place during this time and that cultural values in the United States were in flux. It was an era of violence, rebellion, drug experimentation, and questioning of authority. But it was as if the larger social context around Karl was "shut off" while he was in Catholic school.

As we have said before, the chronosystem has an enormous impact on all the systemic relations described above. We can think of the previous exploration of systems as a snapshot in time of Karl and his relationships—all of which were shifted enormously as the result of his move to public school in the seventh grade. We must remember as well that Karl was developing as a human being during this time. That the transition to public school was made at about twelve years of age is enormously important. Becoming a teenager is full of stresses and strains, even under the best of circumstances.[3] Let us turn now to the ways this cultural formation of Karl affected his experience of the culture of public school.

Karl: Public School's Ritual of Belonging

Sociologist Ann Swidler has suggested that culture "consists of...symbolic vehicles of meaning, including beliefs, ritual practices, art forms, and ceremonies, as well as informal cultural practices such as language, gossip, stories, and rituals of daily life."[4] It is through these symbolic vehicles of meaning that persons and groups make and share meaning over time. This is an important matter to keep in mind regarding Karl's story. He not only changed schools but switched cultures as well. While we may infer that Karl's larger cultural system before public school was flawed at particular levels, it was stable. Karl's stable cultural experience, however, was getting ready to yield to a culture characterized by instability and radical change—brought on by changing schools, combined with the inevitable growing pains of adolescence.

There is every indication in Karl's story that home life stayed just about the same during seventh, eighth, and ninth grades (ages 12–13, 13–14, 14–15). Both parents continued to work long hours. The Catholic church continued to be in the background, though this is not articulated clearly. But gone were the days of protection from social ills in the schooling process. Gone were the blue uniform and black tie (important symbols of belonging in this Catholic school setting). Gone were familiar friends. Gone were religious teachers and priests at school. Gone was the life of an altar boy with its status and rituals. Gone was the safety of routine. Gone was the safety from violence in that school.[5]

Karl put on a new costume or "uniform." How we dress often reflects our sense of self *in context.* If I wear a bathing suit to the seashore, for example, I am wearing a costume that is accepted by others on the beach as normal or acceptable. Nobody would give a second thought to my choice of clothing. But if I wore my bathing suit to Symphony Hall to hear a program of Bach and Mozart, the reaction of those formally dressed persons around me might be one of shock or repulsion.

What did Karl wear into his new context, his new environment? He wore Hush Puppies, skin-tight high-water pants, a Navy peacoat, and a black dickey. It is very likely that Karl's mother knew no more about public school life than he. It is very likely that she got her costuming ideas from the media, from shows such as Happy Days, where the "good boys" dressed like Richie Cunningham. I sense that we can tell much from the mother's image of Karl and her hopes for her son by the way she dressed him for public school. Just imagine the nervousness and expectations of the mother and son on the first day of public school.

Entering a new school can take on ritual dimensions, and Karl's experience was no exception. Within Catholicism, there is a very predictable pattern to confirmation.[6] The confirmand consciously leaves her or his taken-for-granted world and enters a place of prayer, reflection, and study that has been prepared as a sacred space. Very often, the entire parish will pray during Mass for God's blessing on these young persons. The confirmand is asked to make many sacrifices—time, money, priorities, and in some cases the most cherished and valued things in life. All these things are offered to God and to the community of faith as a sign of the seriousness with which the confirmand takes this process of becoming a new person in Christ. There is a time of instruction by the wise persons of the parish, a passing down from one generation to the next the "treasures" of faith.

Then comes a time of disorientation for the confirmand. I have heard both children and adults who have gone through the confirmation process in the Catholic church say that there comes a time when they no longer know exactly who they are or what they are called to do. The ways of the old life (ways of thinking, acting, believing, relating) no longer seem to work. On the other hand, they have great uncertainty about how to go forward. It is a time of emotional struggle, vagueness, and vulnerability.

Then a test is performed by the elders (priest on behalf of the bishop) to see if the confirmand is ready to join the group. If the confirmand is successful, there is a celebration. The confirmand chooses a new name. Special dresses and coats, gifts, a special place in the worship liturgy, and often a special party for the community to celebrate the new member into its midst—a time of many, many "specials." Participation in the Eucharist is the high point of the day. While children in the Catholic church typically make their First Communion in the second grade, Communion is different on this day. A new sense of self and decision is at hand. This is followed by the hardest movement of all, the careful inclusion and integration of the new member into the life of the parish as a person who will begin to prepare to become an elder who will give instruction to new confirmands.[7]

Karl, having grown up in a family with pre-Vatican II religious conviction and practices, would have known this ritual process "in his bones." Karl would have known, at both conscious and unconscious levels, about the power of ritual to transform sense of self and role in the community. But the life-affirming ritual of confirmation that Karl experienced while a student in Catholic school, while almost identical to the ritual process of moving from the culture of the Catholic school to the public school, was quite different in process from what he experienced among his friends at school. But this secular ritual of confirmation by his peers in the new public school was no less powerful in its personal and social dynamics than the ritual process of confirmation in the church. Let us review the "secular confirmation" of Karl by following the nine movements within the ritual process.

Leaving the Taken-for-Granted Places

Karl left the safety of his childhood world. Old friends, places, attitudes, values, ways of relating, ways of greeting, ways of fitting in, became unhelpful in dealing with the new cultural situation.

There was preparation for this leaving process. New clothes, new shoes, new jacket, and new dickey were chosen as appropriate and necessary for the long journey from "here" to "there." All Karl was, all that Karl thought and felt himself to be, were at stake. The once-angelic altar boy was now, in his words, "new, alone, and vulnerable."

Preparation of a New Space

A new space had been prepared, not by the family, school, workplace, peers, or church that Karl knew so well, but by those whom he did not know or understand—and those who did not know or understand him. The public school was a strange world prepared by strangers. Karl was offering himself to the new community, unaware of the cultural patterns extant within it. He had no choice in the matter. His parents decided that this was where he was to attend, and so he complied. It was an economic necessity.

Gathering of the Community

The gathering of the public school community on Karl's behalf was experienced by Karl as a gathering produced by terrorists. Karl was an outsider. He looked odd within this context of new attitudes and values. "After school tonight!" evoked self-doubt, fear, and humiliation. He would try to go home by stealth. He would seek to avoid physical violence. He would try to ignore the words that cut to the quick, but in the end he could not hide from the deep pain of the words. A circle gathered around to meet Karl. Within that circle was "the runt." With the precise organizational technique of a gladiatorial contest, Karl and "the runt" were put in the midst of the human coliseum to fight it out to the death. Karl apparently walked away, no doubt to the taunts of the children turned abusers. It is clear that Karl's humiliation was deep.

At a commencement speech at DePaul University in 1997, Elie Wiesel charged the graduates, "Always remember, my good friends, that there is one sin we must never commit and it is to humiliate another person or to allow another person to be humiliated in our presence without us screaming and shouting and protesting."[8]

Where were Karl's support systems? Where were his parents? Where were his teachers? Where was his church? In his humiliation, he could not disclose his deepest fears to any authority figure. Once, when there was a slight glimmer of hope that a teacher would intervene, there was inaction. Karl was alone in his humiliation and despair. He had no advocates.

Karl's Sacrifice

Karl sacrificed himself—his dignity, his sense of worth—in order to avoid physical violence. He sacrificed his grades. Once a superior student in Catholic school, Karl received D's and F's. He sacrificed his sense that he could take care of himself. He faked getting ill by eating saltines and Alka Seltzer. He sacrificed his social life. He did not go to dances; he did not go to sporting events; he did not go department stores alone—which meant he almost never went. He avoided girls. There was nothing salvific about these sacrifices. Karl was surviving, nothing more. By saving his own life from the fear of physical violence, he was losing it.

Time of Instruction

Karl learned patterns of violence from his father, the case narrative tells us. It is impossible to imagine the pain, humiliation, and embarrassment of taking a Brillo pad to his home-crafted tattoo. Karl learned the way of the bully from the bullies in school. There is no indication that any academic learning of any significant sort was taking place in the public school for Karl. But as Karl's anger moved to uncontrollable rage, he was learning the ways of violence through the behavior of his tormentors. Clearly not prepared by any adult or social setting (such as the family or the church) to deal with bullies, Karl took notice of the ways of violence. The bullies were consistent in their desire to be in relation with Karl, but only by means of violence. The relationship had but one purpose, but one outcome—the death of the other as person. Karl was being pushed, in this way, to death.

Karl's Time of Disorientation

Of all the movements of ritual we have discussed thus far, this is by all means the most heartbreaking. Clearly, there is no indication that Karl was conscious of his decision to become a man who would take on the behavior of gross violence, physical and emotional. The decision came in an instant, when the unbearable anger that had been controlled for so long finally exploded in rage-filled vengeance and power. He did not belong to either culture anymore. He stopped caring. His spirit had been broken under the weight of violence. He felt little regard for himself or others. He did not feel that things would ever change. He felt oppression. He felt humiliation. He felt abandoned by authority figures. And in a flash, in an unconscious release of rage, he became a man of violence. As a bully now, the only relation he wanted with his persecutors was death. The pleasures of violence and the power of violence were ineffective in dealing with the bullies around him. Why do I say ineffective? Did not the bullies now flee in terror from the threat or action of his power? I say ineffective because violence did not heal Karl nor those whom he violated. Nothing was transformed. "Creatures that were once men," in the words of novelist Maxim Gorky, were eliminated, but emotional and physical pain endured for Karl.[9]

Karl's Test

The details of the case narrative are shocking, disturbing, repulsive, and heartrending. Karl became the very epitome of the very persons he feared and abhorred. Ripping gums from mouths, slamming heads on desks, sexually abusing girls, shoplifting, smoking in defiance of authority figures in school, sniffing glue, drinking, stealing cars, and assaulting his own father are but some of the acts unleashed in that fateful moment of decision to strike back. Karl finally fit into the public school that he had entered in the seventh grade. But he wasn't Richie Cunningham, nor was he himself. He had passed the test that the bullies had set before him, but at the cost of his own identity.

Karl's Celebration

As curious as it may at first seem, the judge at his last sentencing hearing performed the celebration of Karl's success at violence. Rather than being placed in a correctional facility, Karl chose a military career. Eight arrests and five convictions left few options. I suspect it was a somber celebration, as Karl's reflections would indicate. Guarding a checkpoint in Vietnam is a powerful metaphor of Karl's final success. And it gave him no satisfaction. He knew that he had engaged in this life of violence as his only known means of self-defense. He knew of no other options. Karl knew as well that his solution to the problem of bullying had been inadequate. While the school bullies sashayed their way to the prom, Karl guarded a checkpoint thousands of miles from home. Once again, Karl's cultural environment had changed. Once again, he did not choose his new context; it was chosen for him. Once again, he did not belong where he found himself.

Integration into the Community as Elder

Karl was successful in his learning at the public school. He fit in. He had a new name, and it was Terror. He could defend himself physically from anyone. He could be popular—but only within the context of that public school. There was no going back. Graduation had taken place. The prom was over. The ritual that Karl experienced succeeded and failed. Karl was ready to face a life of violence in the public school. But public school no longer existed for Karl. Karl's experience of violence at the hands of bullies, and his experience of violence at his own hand prepared him for a school culture that he was no longer part of. He found himself in the military. He saw the limits of such a life. What was he going to do next, and how?

In answer to my question about praying for the bullies, Karl is resolute—he will never forgive them.

Funding Events in Life

During our lives, certain events are of such significance that they shape our interpretation of life in profound and deep ways. This is no less true for a twelve-year-old reflecting on the significance of an important event that occurred at age four than it is for a forty-two-year-old reflecting on events that happened at twelve.[10] We make sense of ourselves, others, and the world by remembering. These significant events may be understood as "funding events" (events that provide powerful images with long-lasting significance) that naturally, and often unconsciously, become those places our imaginations turn to make sense of the present. As we grow older, we may find that we reinterpret our lives and the significances of our funding events. As we age, we may seek to resolve some of the questions or hurts that are imbedded in the funding events themselves. But the funding events of our lives, those deep places of meaning and self-understanding, tend to stay with us for a lifetime. These funding events, more often than not, can become places of entrapment and stagnation—or places of reflection, positive growth, and transformation.

Bullying between the seventh and ninth grades is a funding event of deep significance for forty-two-year-old Karl. Violence suffered day after day, week after week, and year after year at the hands of bullies creates an area of deep hurt and unresolved anger. I have known persons who are perplexed about the way some of their friends in middle age continue to talk about events in their lives that happened one or two decades ago. The energy, both positive and negative, produced by funding events can last many years, or even a lifetime. It has been said that the human psyche is not bound by time, and it is true.

We forget sometimes how violent children can be to other children. It is not a pleasant topic, and shatters our romanticized vision of what childhood ought to be. There are some who seek to trace such violence back to parents, others back to peers, and still others to the ways in which the child takes responsibility for meaning-making as she or he grows up.[11] No single approach is adequate, and the truth lurks somewhere among and below these strategies. Was Karl's response to these bullies conditioned by his alcoholic father? Was Karl's lack of constructive attachment to his mother a factor? Were the peers available in the public school adequate for Karl's success as a teenager? Why could Karl not count on those crucial authority figures in his life to be his advocates? Where were the parents, the neighbors, the priests, the peers, the teachers, the school staff? Why did Karl not go to his parents for help? Who were these bullies? Where did they come from? What became of them? The ways in which Karl engaged the world of the public school offers no easy answers. Even Bronfenbrenner's bioecological model, as helpful as it is in the description of Karl's relational support system, does not give answers about this complex person.

We do know some things with certainty. Karl moved into the new school unprepared for its challenges. His support systems were weak, if not nonexistent. He was humiliated by the bullies. He ultimately humiliated the bullies. At forty-two, the experience of violence for three years as an awakening teenager continued to fund Karl's emotional energy and interpretation of life. Retaliatory violence did not solve the hurt and pain that Karl experienced. The case stands as a testimony to the futility, waste, and powerlessness of violence and to its lasting effects on the human soul.

Summary

As adults, we have all been bullied and we have all bullied others. Karl's narrative is extreme in its violence, and that excess allows us to see some of the patterns of bullying more clearly. We have noticed that relational support systems, so crucial to all growing persons, were deeply flawed or absent. We regret the absence in Karl's life of adults who offered protection and/or advocacy. The ritual process of becoming a new member of a group, so essential particularly during adolescence, failed to prepare Karl for life in his new school, or for life anywhere else. Karl was silent about his experience of violence at first, telling nobody about his situation (at least not directly). A once successful young boy became a failure. When Karl took on the life of violence in order to stop violence against him, his life became more hellish than before. His life was out of control, only to be saved by one person who seemed to take his crisis seriously, in this case a courtroom judge, a stranger.[12] The promise of being in relation with others, the gift of being created in God's image, was inverted and perverted. Instead of joy, relationship brought agony and self-degradation.

This moving story of bullying prepares us to enter the next chapter of this book, in which bullying is placed more directly in conversation with the understanding of doxology and sin introduced in chapter 1. Constructive alternatives to bullying are discussed.

CHAPTER 3

Bullying as Spiritual Crisis

To this point, we have explored the origins and consequences of violence. We have followed the story of one man's personal experience with the violence of bullying. We went from a general discussion of violence in chapter 1 to a specific example of violence in chapter 2. In this chapter, we engage the first two chapters in conversation with each other.

So many definitions and understandings of bullying are in the popular media right now. *Bullying* seems to have become a catchall word for all kinds of violence. It is my evaluation that much called "bullying" in the popular media and press is not bullying at all. It sometimes seems that all forms of senseless violence are acts of bullying, but this is not true. If, as Christian parents, teachers, and religious leaders, we are going to begin to take bullying seriously, it is necessary to know what we mean by "bullying." This chapter begins with a very condensed definition of bullying, which provides us with a very helpful "shorthand" for remembering what bullying is.

Let us start by defining bullying concretely, based on our reading of chapters 1 and 2. We then look at a dominant social myth about human relatedness that pervades (and deforms) any discussion of empathy, the social myth of tolerance. We discover in the following discussion of empathy why tolerance is an ineffective basis for reflection and action in our world today. We then return to Karl's story in light of these discussions, in order to understand the depth of bullying as a spiritual crisis.

What Is Bullying?

Bullying is a behavioral manifestation of spiritual crisis in which an individual bully or group of bullies seeks relation with another person or persons through repeated acts of violence over time. The behaviors of bullying are intended to hurt and disturb others. These acts of violence may be physical and/or emotional (threatened or carried out). An imbalance of power always exists between the bully and the bullied. Bullying can take place by individuals, informal groups of persons, formal organizations, or nations.

In the most significant study of bullying in the United States to date, a team of researchers that included Tonja R. Nansel, Mary Overpect, Ramani S. Pilla, W. June Ruan, and others began with an observation that is almost beyond belief. They wrote, "Although violence among U.S. youth is a current major concern, bullying is infrequently addressed and no national data on the prevalence of bullying is available."[1] To date, there is only one longitudinal research article in Christian religious education written on the topic of bullying.[2]

If violence among children is of general concern in the United States, how can it be that so little research exists about bullying? My deep sense is that violence is viewed as acceptable and inevitable by most adults, including adults in the church. If a class on the topic of children and teenagers and sex is offered in the local congregation, one can rest assured of a packed audience. If a class on the topic of children and teenagers and violence is offered in the local congregation, it is likely that only a very few persons will attend.[3] More often than not, the church politely ignores the depths of the violence of bullying within its daily practices, outside the walls of its community, and beyond its national borders. When the violence of bullying is addressed, such violence is something that is a problem for "others"—not for those within the worshiping congregation. But we know through experience that bullying takes place on church staffs, in church educational settings, and among parish members of all ages.[4] I am reminded of the opening line of the book for children about bullying entitled *Nobody Knew What to*

Do: A Story About Bullying, which reads, "Nobody likes to think about it, even though we know it is not okay to hurt a person."[5]

Research Related to Bullying

Publication by *The Journal of the American Medical Association* on April 25, 2001, of the article "Bullying Behaviors Among U.S. Youth: Prevalence and Association with Psychosocial Adjustment," signaled a new era in bully research in the United States.[6] The results of this innovative research were sobering. The study found that 29.9% of the children involved in the study reported moderate or frequent involvement in bullying; 13% reported that they were the bully; 10.6% reported that they were bullied; and 6.3% reported that they were both the bully and the bullied. The survey included national representation from children in the United States in grades six through ten. The data was collected in 1998, and the analytic sample included 15,686 students.

The national estimate of bullying, based on the data collected from the research, is staggering. It is estimated that some 1,681,030 children from grades six through ten bully other children once a week or more. Some 1,611,809 children, according to this estimate process, are bullied once a week or more. What specific types of bullying were addressed in this research? The types of bullying included belittling about religion and race; belittling about physical appearance or speech; hitting, slapping, or pushing; spreading rumors; and making sexual comments and/or gestures. One can imagine other forms of bullying that take place, such as shunning; silencing; demanding money; making threats, including threatening to hurt other people; or name-calling. Compelling evidence exists that gay children are special targets of bullies.[7]

These significant findings may be related to other research projects, both in the United States and outside the United States. An Australian study published in 2001, for example, concluded that "low self-concept may trigger troublemaking behavior in a possibly successful attempt to enhance subsequent self-concept."[8] Doubtless the bully feels a success in the practice of violence that he or she may not experience in other relational contexts. This same study concluded that victims of bullying were those whose self-concept was low. That the bully and the victim of bullying both may have a low self-concept is noteworthy. The bully, it would appear, is more socially apt than the bullied person.[9] It is certainly not uncommon for bullies to have many friends, followers, and admirers.[10] Moreover, the bullied person tends to be smaller or physically weaker than the bully. Bullied children tend to be insecure, anxious, depressed, lonely, and unhappy. A recent Australian study of nearly three thousand teenagers makes a convincing correlation between ongoing bullying and depression.[11]

In the United States, the National Threat Assessment Center of the Secret Service concluded that almost two-thirds of the thirty-seven school shootings over the past twenty-five years were the result of persons seeking vengeance who felt "persecuted, bullied, threatened, attacked, or injured." It was the conclusion of this study that the persons who attacked schools had been bullied severely for a long time.[12]

In my own research, I conclude that the bully may be a popular and charismatic leader. The bully may work alone, in groups, or through other persons. Quite often the bully has excellent organizational skills. Bullies tend to be a little older than those they bully. Bullies tend to be bigger and stronger than average, though this does not hold true in gangs of bullies. Bullies tend to be aggressive and impulsive. Bullies are low in empathy and generally uncaring, though they may have learned ways of "conning" adults into the belief that they are angels. I have found that in many cases, persons who were bullies as children do not remember—nor do they realize—how they caused other persons pain for a lifetime. They have little sense of the feelings of others, or that their behavior may have consequences for others.[13] Bullies do not very often like school. The connection between bullying and revenge, so much a part of Karl's story, is of special concern to those persons interested in public health. Curiously, virtually no study on the relation between bullying and revenge exists in any literature.[14] Several studies indicate that girls tend to internalize aggression, while boys tend to externalize aggression.[15] "High target" children of aggression are more likely to internalize aggression than to seek help from others or engage in problem solving.[16]

It is likely that a child in a badly functioning family system is more likely to become a bully or a victim of bullying than a child from a healthily functioning family system. The bullied child frequently has few friends, has low self-concept, and is introverted, timid, and nonassertive. In many cases, the bullied child is physically weaker than her or his peers. Increasingly, studies that focus on bullying include the bully, the victim, and the bystander. Many times, teachers or other adults will be frightened of the behavior of the bully—and choose to ignore the violence. Those who witness bullying and do nothing about it have, in effect, sanctioned the behavior.[17] In many cases, it is possible that persons who witness the violence of bullying may themselves feel violated, or may identify with the violence of the bully.[18] There is no such thing as a neutral bystander.

Many factors, as Bronfenbrenner has helped us imagine, are related to the ways in which persons develop over time. Even at that, Bronfenbrenner no doubt scratches at the surface of the complexities of being and becoming human. At the same time, the importance of the macrosystem, which includes dominant myths, narratives, attitudes, and ideologies of culture, provides some concrete clues to the ways persons adapt and respond to the social systems into which they are socialized. One of the dominant social myths of the West, increasingly exported in this postmodern era of globalization, is the myth of tolerance. It is my contention that toleration provdes a firm ground for violence between persons and groups in its very attempt to promote peace. Moreover, the socially accepted norm of tolerance inevitably gives rise to violence and the sanction of bullying. So let us start our analysis of bullying by turning our attention to the meaning and implications of tolerance in our times.

The Social Myth of Tolerance

We are the myths we live. Myths are those stories in culture that give our lives and actions meaning. Sometimes we are conscious of these myths, but most of the time they form the unconscious taken-for-granted narratives that define us. Tolerance forms the basis of one of those cultural myths that define us, especially in the West, but one that we think about very little. Tolerance is a pervasive and powerful idea in our culture. It may seem awkward to question its value in public; it may even seem un-American. That is a testimony to the behavioral power of social myths. But I contend that tolerance is an inadequate and destructive way for persons to be in relation with one another. I contend that the cultural myth of tolerance sets the stage for bullying and for violence. We know that intolerance is destructive to the practice of Christian diversity. But the opposite of intolerance is not tolerance; it is empathy. Tolerance as an end results in intolerance. Intolerance in the end leads to violence. In order to understand the inadequacy of tolerance in regard to diversity for our day, let us go back for a moment to the Enlightenment.

The Enlightenment is *the* crucial historical event in the West for understanding the social myth of tolerance. The Enlightenment's lessons about living together in a pluralistic world are ones we continue to exercise in the West (and increasingly at a global level), consciously or unconsciously. Whatever else the Enlightenment was, it was a peacemaking movement. We forget today that the Thirty Years War (1618–48) was a powerful, pervasive memory for people in the West all the way up to World War I. Following the Wars of Religion after the Reformation, the Thirty Years War was based on religious pluralism that could not see its way to peace. In the name of God, Europe sought to destroy the "other," and exhausted itself—by the time of the Treaty of Westfalia—in violence.

The politically liberal virtue of tolerance that emerged out of the carnage of the Wars of Religion and the Thirty Years War arose from the experiences of religious hatred and war. What does this have to do with the violence of bullying? The social myth of tolerance has been accepted as a positive and good thing for human relations for almost four hundred years in the West. Tolerance of persons who are different than "us" has stopped conflict in many instances. But the live-and-let-live values embedded in the notion of tolerance do not promote communication, mutual respect, and caring. Tolerance creates walls of separation and diminished communication that breed intolerance—lack of mutual understanding, lack of communication, lack of mutual respect, and lack of caring. Tolerance may be understood as a form of force that turns the tolerated person, group, or nation into a thing. A relationship of toleration is a relationship of distrust, misunderstanding, stereotype, envy, and fear. A relationship of toleration is a relationship of an imbalance of power. Tolerance is a way of being in relation with the other person or group that denies the value of diversity, that perpetuates a sense of superiority, and that paves the road to attempted mutual destruction in times of scarcity. Muslims and Christians tolerated each other for years in Sarajevo. Palestinians and Jews tolerate each other at times in the Middle East. Bullies tolerate others as they seek to be in relation with them, but toleration simply intensifies the felt need to disregard the true humanity of others. Toleration is a sign of personal and social dysfunction. Toleration is a sign of the fear of diversity.

Joan Wallach Scott, a professor of social science at the Institute for Advanced Study in Princeton, New Jersey, has suggested that "differences may be what we have most in common."[19] While Scott is writing with the modern university in mind, the implications for settings such as home, school, and church are worth exploring. If, in our individual and group situations of everyday living, we were to begin with the notion that differences are what we have most in common and that differences are not an exception to the rule, but the rule of all human relating, our self-understanding and the understanding of groups by one another would take on a new focus. Tolerance begins with the opposite assumption — that what we have most in common is our commonality.

The theme of tolerance is one of the most hotly debated areas of political science today. If a person lives in the United States or other Western (or Western-dominated) context, it is impossible not to know the expected behavioral patterns of tolerance—whether conscious or unconscious. Stephen Kautz at Emory University in Atlanta, Georgia, begins by affirming that "tolerance is a liberal virtue."[20] He continues:

> Beginning with Rousseau, even more or less friendly critics of liberal politics wondered: What is the real effect on the souls of human beings on the practice of the liberal freedoms? Do liberal citizens commonly display the complementary virtues of independence and self-restraint that liberal philosophy commends?[21]

Philosopher Richard Rorty answers Kautz. He suggests that liberals "have become so open- minded that our brains have fallen out," and that liberals have lost "any capacity for moral indignation, any capacity to feel contempt."[22] Herbert Marcuse took the criticism of tolerance, a keystone of liberalism, even further. Marcuse concluded that toleration is essentially an ideology of oppression, giving only the appearance of relation with freedom. He wrote harshly that

> Today tolerance appears again as what it was in its origins, at the beginning of the modern period—a partisan goal, a subversive liberating notion and practice. Conversely, what is proclaimed and practiced as tolerance today, is in many of its most effective manifestations serving the cause of oppression.[23]

Lest we conclude that only "liberals" are quick to point out the limitations of a liberal and Enlightenment-based understanding of tolerance, it is well to include two examples of such critique from what might be called "conservative" Christian voices. Bruce W. Speck, a professor of English at the University of Memphis, for example, contends that "many people claim that they are relativists and proponents of tolerance. Yet relativism cannot foster tolerance in part because it is untenable as a coherent philosophy."[24] Or take David Hollenbach, a Jesuit priest, who concludes that

> The standard response to the diversity of groups and value systems in Western political culture has long been an appeal to the virtue of tolerance. Tolerance is a live-and-let-live attitude that avoids introducing conceptions of the full human good into political discourse...If my analysis is correct, [tolerance] actually further threatens democracy by deepening alienation and anomie... when the pluralism of diverse groups veers toward a state of group conflict with racial or class or religious dimensions, pure tolerance can become a strategy like that of the ostrich with its head in the sand.[25]

Feminist researchers have concluded often that this understanding of tolerance voiced by Hollenbach is essentially correct. For example, the research of Eleanor R. Hall, Judith Howard, and Sherrie L. Boezio has investigated the issue of rape tolerance. They conclude that "the relationship between tolerance of rape and sexist attitudes was stronger than the relationship between tolerance of rape and an antisocial personality."[26] The researchers demonstrate convincingly how popularized notions of tolerance that work at a commonsense or even preconscious level shape the attitudes of persons at all levels of society—and how these attitudes may reach to the deepest levels of our thinking and acting. As historian Henry F. May has noted, the Enlightenment "was too deeply embodied in the American institutions and habits of thought to be abandoned altogether."[27]

What can these representative approaches to the limits of tolerance tell us? (1) Tolerance is a description of the relation of persons in societal contexts where there is a presumed diversity of cultures and religions. (2) Something about tolerance seems to undermine, rather than strengthen, the societal notion of democracy. And yet tolerance was developed for democracy's good. But this hope seems not to have worked out in practice. (3) The language of tolerance is a language of power relations. Who shall be tolerated is, in the last analysis, a choice of those in power. (4) The limits of tolerance seem unclear. (5) The ground on which tolerance bases its life seems inadequate for the common good. In fact, it appears that tolerance would deny the possibility of a common good. (6) If we stand back and observe "tolerance as practiced," we see a surprising number of unlikely people who are convinced of its inherent limits—feminists, conservative Christians, postmodern philosophers, and social radicals. All these social critics presume that diversity is a permanent quality of our life together and conclude that tolerance is not "working." Yet the myth of tolerance continues to be espoused by leading educators in the United States.

John Rawls, professor of philosophy at Harvard University, is one of the most eloquent spokespersons of toleration for political process in the United States today. He accepts "the fact of pluralism," and simultaneously looks forward to "social unity for a democratic society."[28] He is eloquent in his formulation of the interconnection of "society's main political, social and economic institutions, and how they fit into one unified scheme of public cooperation."[29] Rawls suggests that "society's main institutions, together with the accepted forms of their interpretation, are seen as a fund of implicitly shared fundamental ideas and principles."[30] Rawls concludes that what he calls "overlapping consensus" is possible between groups very different from one another. What allows consensus is a shared sense of what counts as justice and fairness.[31] Upon what is this idea of overlapping consensus built? Rawls reflects that it is "the virtues of tolerance and being ready to meet others halfway, and the virtue of reasonableness and the sense of fairness."[32]

For me, Rawls has articulated a careful and constructively critical restatement of the liberal tradition for our times. Yet the interplay of overlapping consensus and tolerance only exacerbates the critiques of tolerance that are hotly debated today. Such an elegant model undermines the play of diversity in important ways. The play of diversity, which requires dialogue for the good of all, is diluted. Contact between different groups comes only at points of overlapping consensus related to issues of justice. One can imagine in this model that diverse groups function best if they tend to stay away from one another in daily affairs. Diverse groups will tend to find points of agreement not through dialogue, but through coincidental areas of agreement. This process of what might be called managed diversity (with the state playing a "neutral role")[33] by maintaining an essentially traditional liberal understanding of toleration, misses the opportunity to engage in the play of diversity. As political scientist Susan Mendus has noted,

> Autonomy-based liberalism ultimately contains no commitment to the value of diversity in and of itself. It

justifies only those diverse forms of life which themselves value autonomy and thus makes toleration a pragmatic device—a temporary expedient—not a matter of principle.[34]

Where does all this leave us as we consider the topic of bullying as a spiritual crisis? What we hold dear as a people in the West, and particularly in political and social practice in the United States, this toleration, has an inherent flaw. Toleration as practiced gives social support and sanction to the inevitability of violence, of which bullying is one public manifestation. The end goal of toleration as practiced in the United States is the elimination of the diversity of persons through the isolation of diverse groups. Toleration is acceptance of a worldview—more often than not by social absorption or assimilation than by systematical learning—that had its origins in the Enlightenment. Understandings of self and autonomy, privacy, religion, science, community, diversity, power (especially as it relates to forms of totalitarianism), the state and neutrality, justice, and the common good that arise from this complex discussion, form—in one way or another—an ethical vision that shapes our habits of daily life.

Joan Wallach Scott's affirmation of diversity in unity is very different from the liberal understanding of unity in diversity.[35] The possibility that toleration may be used as a form of social oppression, that it leads to isolation and anomie,[36] that a common good is ultimately beyond its limits, are contrary to the themes of hospitality, friendship, and empathy. It is within the Western cultural assumption of toleration that we now turn to empathy and the violence of bullying.

Empathy as Christian Practice

Bullying embodies a pattern of behavior in which empathy is malformed. Lucinda A. Stark Huffaker suggests that sin is "the failure of empathy."[37] Empathy as a way of being and knowing self, others, and the natural world is the essential core of Christian hospitality, of the ability to recognize the "other" or "the stranger" as fully human. Empathy is not merely sympathy[38], but a profound recognition of the other as other. Where there is no empathy, where there is no concerned suffering in the presence of the other, there are the seeds of violence. Where there is no empathy, there can be no "other."

Where there is no empathy, there can be no forgiveness, no caring. Empathy is a religious practice—imagining the other person or group of persons as truly human, created by God, "of putting yourself in" another person's "shoes, not in order to wear them as your own but in order to have some understanding of why someone else might want to wear them,"[39] of opening oneself to the possibility of entering into the suffering of the other person.

Theologian Edward Farley writes in his book *Divine Empathy: A Theology of God* that "empathy, concerned suffering is a participation in the life of the genuine other" and is a description of the nature of God.[40] Farley continues, "Thus, in Jesus, relation to God and empathetic concern come to the same thing."[41] To affirm the life of the genuine other, with concern and a willingness to participate in the life of the genuine other is not only a manifestation of doxology in a person's life but an affirmation of who God is for us in the world. Our relations with ourselves, with others, and with God are at stake here. To engage in the spiritual discipline of empathy is to participate in the life of God in an embodied way. Biblical scholar Jon L. Berquist has put it this way: "This embodied God is a being of passion and compassion…God yearns for people. God desires contact and real relationship. God makes choices and takes risks as part of living life with people. God wants to live next to us humans and will move heaven and earth themselves to make it happen. This embodied God is vibrant, alive, and powerful."[42]

What has all of this to do with a bully? The bully enacts a cycle of violence that has at its deepest levels a desire to be in relation with the other. But the bully's correct desire to be in relation with the other has been distorted by sin. What the bully desires most, intimate relation with the other, is what becomes most elusive. Tragically, the bully may not know of any other way of life or any other options available than this self-negating process. Very often the bully is born into a social context that is entrapped by practices of sin. From the earliest years the development of empathy is deprived of its life-giving nature and function. We know that empathy begins to express itself naturally in most children at around eighteen months, perhaps earlier in some cases.[43] This emergence of empathy is a mysterious expression and reminder of what it means to be created in the image of God.

Where there is no empathy, where there is no suffering in the presence of the other, there are the seeds of violence. Where there is no empathy, there can be no caring. The bully has keen empathic skills without empathy. She or he is able to imagine, to intuit what the other is feeling—more often than not with amazing precision. To "read" the other person is an empathic skill. But the person "read" is an object because the self itself is an isolated object—but with a deep yearning to feel and be in relation with self and other. Through acts of violence, the bully is able to transcend isolation and belong—but only for a brief moment. It is as if violence provides energy powerful enough to break through the durable defenses of self-isolation and self-protection that allow life to continue on a daily basis.

Violence is not only the illusion of relation, but is in fact relation, without empathy or sympathy or caring. It is ultimately more isolating, more numbing, but it is a signal of the spiritual longing to be in relation with another. For the bully, violence is one of the few ways that pleasure is experienced, however fleetingly, that relation with the other is experienced. This experience of being in relation with the other may be described as hate or rage or contempt. It is a living hell, because through violence the person becomes more and more isolated.

Violence is addictive. It gives intense momentary pleasure. And like any drug, violence must increase in order to repeat the sensation of intimacy with the other that was once experienced, which was once felt. To be a bully is to be a person in deep self-destructive spiritual crisis. The path of the bully who desires to be in relation with the other is to destroy the other, which leaves the bully in utter desolation. We may find this understanding of the bully frighteningly horrible, for we know that the bully may be an individual, a group of persons, or even a national phenomenon. Two years before his murder, Oscar Romero, Catholic bishop of El Salvador, connected this tragic cycle of violence to the death of an individual/death of self. His words, which would summarize his own martyrdom, focus on the violence-revealing consequence of every unjust death.

> We know that the death of an individual is an offense against God. We know that such sin really is mortal, not only in the sense of the interior death of the person who commits the sin, but also because of the real, objective death that sin produces.[44]

Frequently the bullied person becomes dependent on the very person who violates her or him. Both the bully and the bullied share the condition of spiritual crisis. It seems that the more violent and harsh the relation between the bullied and the bully, the more durable the dysfunctional relationship becomes. Such a violent dependency is reinforced by both the bullied person's and the bully's inherent desires to be in relation—yet deformed by the abuse of power exercised by the bully. More often than not, the power over the bullied person by the bully is so significantly violent that death itself is the only option for the bully and for the victim who (finally) seeks to break the cycle of violence. The bully, in her or his desire to be in relation with others, destroys all that is not herself or himself. The only person left to brutalize when all others have been destroyed is oneself. The bullying of oneself is the tragic and ultimate consequence of being alone.

"Why did this person stay in such an abusive relationship?" is a question heard often that barely masks disdain for a victim of bullying. This is particularly true if the victim is female. Such a question underestimates the inequality extant in raw and violent power over another person, and the instinctive desire on the part of the bullied person to survive emotionally and physically. There is no room here to blame the bully or the bullied person, who coexist in a destructive pattern of violence and death. The relation of the bully and the victim is too complex for understanding one or the other as "good" or "evil." There is only room to affirm life and the possibility of change in the midst of sin.

Bullying is a form of inward spiritual crisis expressed outwardly. Those who bully are created in the image of God and yearn to be in relation with other persons and with God. Bullies embody violence as the means by which relationships are established. Bullies may act as individuals or groups of individuals. As a form of spiritual crisis, bullying is the way a person may seek to be in relation with the other person and/or with God repeatedly—with the mistaken sense that somehow a relation can be established through violence.

Bullying is repeated violence. As terrible as a single act of violence may be, bullying is a pattern of repeated violence over time. Bullying more often than not includes physical violence toward the victim. Bullies consciously or unconsciously engage in acts of violence against others, but are likely unconscious of the reason why this form of destructive or self-destructive behavior has been chosen. Bullying more often than not will include both physical and psychological patterns of violence and domination. Practical theologian Carol Lakey Hess has defined spirituality "as the practice of remembering, and at times rediscovering, our center in God."[45] A spirituality of violence, in its inherent desire to remember its center, flings the center further and further beyond its grasp. Or in the words of poet William Butler Yeats, "Things fall apart; the center cannot hold."[46]

Bullying more often than not gives pleasure to the bully. The pleasure of being in relation with others in the role of bully, however, is fleeting and momentary. Acts of violence must be repeated and must become more intense over time to satisfy the human hunger for relation. The bully's victim is often destroyed in this life-robbing process, and the bully has no other option than to find another victim(s), or to victimize herself or himself.

Frequently a bully will insist that he or she is entitled to bully other persons. Persons who believe that others exist to serve them embody an "entitlement of abuse." This oppression of the other person in the name of entitlement is a common form of bullying that involves power as related to economic level, social status, race, religion, age, nationality, and gender. It is not unrelated in attitude and practice to the old English servant system of the manor house, or to the pattern of life experienced by European colonizers in Africa and India. A perceived natural inevitability of superiority orders the world by those who believe they are *entitled*. A brief story may help illustrate this situation.

In a local public elementary school located next to a major and prestigious research university, a second-grade teacher took her class to the cafeteria for lunch. Two well-to-do caucasian boys in the class, both children of faculty members at the university, had the habit of making racist and snide remarks about the Caribbean black man who worked in the cafeteria cleaning almost-emptied food trays as the children finished eating. The teacher of these boys, in the bustle of the meal, knew nothing of the comments made by the boys about the man. One day the teacher happened to be walking by the food tray dropoff point and heard the boys' comments.

The teacher immediately took the two boys aside and asked them to repeat the words that they had spoken. The boys repeated the slurs, oblivious to the possibility that the man would be affected by them. The teacher asked how long they had been engaged in this practice, and the boys replied, "Since the beginning of the year." For more than three months, the boys had been using abusive language toward the man in the cafeteria.

The teacher took the two boys over to the man and asked him, "Have you heard what these boys have been saying to you?" The man replied that he had heard the comments and repeated some of them in the presence of the boys and the teacher. The teacher asked, "How do these comments make you feel?" The man replied that he felt angry, hurt, and humiliated. In an instant, one child began to sob the words, "I'm sorry!" while the other boy stood with drooping head.

But the story does not end here. On hearing what the teacher had done with the boys in the cafeteria, the parents of one of the children made an appointment for a conference. During the conference the parents criticized the teacher: "It was not your place to embarrass my child like that. After all, the custodian is an adult. If he had had a problem with the comments of my child, he should have been a man and said something. I don't know why you are bothering my son. It is the man's problem, not my son's. If you insist on harassing my child in this way, I will have my lawyer contact your principal." This true story is illustrative of the bullying of entitlement, a form of violence more common than any of us would like to acknowledge. It is worthy of note that both the family and the custodian had been at the school for three years, but for this family the custodian was a "thing."

Empathy is the essential core of hospitality, of the ability to recognize the "other" as fully human. Hospitality is not interested in the domination of power relations found in entitlement. Hospitality is concerned with the integrity, mutuality, and gift of diversity. With this recognition comes suffering. Where there is no empathy, where there is no suffering in the presence of the other, there are the seeds of violence. Where there is no empathy, there can be no "other." Where there is no empathy, there can be no "self."

Teaching Empathy

How do we teach empathy? I am more and more convinced we teach empathy most effectively by modeling it ourselves in our relations with others. I am finding that for many children and adults, their lives have been turned from violence, prejudice, racism, and hatred by the act of another child or another adult being willing to suffer with them in their painful isolation. Sometimes empathy takes the form of confrontation in love and justice. In a very unusual story in the book of Matthew, Jesus encounters a Canaanite woman. The story reads this way:

> Jesus left that place and went away to the district of Tyre and Sidon. Just then a Canaanite woman from that region came out and started shouting, "Have mercy on me, Lord, Son of David; my daughter is tormented by a demon." But he did not answer her at all. And his disciples came and urged him, saying, "Send her away, for she keeps shouting

after us." He answered, "I was sent only to the lost sheep of the house of Israel." But she came and knelt before him, saying, "Lord, help me." He answered, "It is not fair to take the children's food and throw it to the dogs." She said, "Yes, Lord, yet even the dogs eat the crumbs that fall from their masters' table." Then Jesus answered her, "Woman, great is your faith! Let it be done for you as you wish." And her daughter was healed instantly (Mt. 15:21–28).

This biblical passage has been interpreted in many different ways. But what I would like to focus on is the relation between Jesus and the Canaanite woman. Historically, Jews despised, avoided, and hated Canaanites as disposable, idol-worshiping heathens. The best thing to do with them was to force them out so that Jews could occupy their lands. When the Palestinian Jew, Jesus, was confronted by a Canaanite, the possibility for religious, racial, and ethnic hatred to surface was real. Add the fact that this was a woman, and the scene is set. The disciples tell her to leave, and they embody the violence they have learned from generations of hate and prejudice.

Even Jesus implies she is a "dog." One commentary suggests that Jesus' use of the word "dog" is really not all that bad. After all, the "diminutive form" of the word "dog" was used.[47] "You little dog" does not seem to help the situation much.[48] Jesus as xenophobic racist is a hard pill to swallow. Sam Keen correctly concludes in *Faces of the Enemy*, "Before we enter into warfare or genocide, we first dehumanize those we mean to 'eliminate'."[49] Just a little dog. But in a moment of enormous strength, dignity, nonviolence, and wisdom brimming with suffering, the Canaanite woman sympathetically throws up to Jesus a mirror in which to see the dehumanizing force of his own words, not as an act of retribution, but as embodiment of a caring and empathetic teacher who believes so deeply in the necessity of interdependence, including interdependence with the Palestinian Jew, that she is willing to perish for it. And remarkably, Jesus sees himself. Through the eyes of a nonperson, Jesus sees himself, repents, and learns more fully what it means to be a caring and just human.[50]

In the words of pastoral caregiver Marie McCarthy, "Empathy creates an environment where it is safe to know and to not know, where it is safe to explore, make mistakes, be uncertain, where it is possible to see things in new ways."[51] Within the play of difference, a safe environment necessarily includes constructive, often life-changing conflict. Through confrontation, the Canaanite woman created a safe environment where Jesus could see his hate, where Jesus could move beyond violence, where Jesus could know the Canaanite woman as fully human, and from which Jesus could leave transformed. Jesus and the Canaanite woman were engaged in radical dialogue that afforded an expanded understanding of religion, including a redefinition of self in relation to others.

Empathy as a Way of Knowing

How is empathy a form of knowing? In and through empathy, we learn the basis for a healthy and life-giving interdependence in our diversities. According to H. Edward Everding and Lucinda A. Huffaker, "empathy is not only an important quality of the 'holding environment' that is conducive to growth, but it is also recognized as a conduit for self-development through the experience of 'holding' others."[52]

Without the disposition of empathy, it is impossible to care. Just as empathy is a way of knowing, so also is caring. Just as empathy is a form of radical dialogue, so also is caring. Perhaps more than anyone else, Nel Noddings has helped educators consider the central role of caring in our communities of learning. For me, the most helpful aspect of Noddings's work is what she calls the relation between "the one caring" and "the cared for." She writes eloquently that to be in relation with the cared for

> maintains and enhances the relatedness that is funda-
> mental to human reality and, in education, it sets the stage
> for the teacher's effort in maintaining and increasing the
> child's receptive capacity. As the teacher receives the child
> and works with him on cooperatively designed projects,
> as she resists the temptation—or the mandate—to
> manipulate the child, to squeeze him into some mold, she
> ·establishes a climate of receptivity. The one caring reflects
> reality as she sees it to the child. She accepts him as she
> hopes he will accept himself—seeing what is there,
> considering what might be changed, speculating on what
> might be.[53]

Within communities of diversity, caring for one another, caring for self, and caring for the world are mandatory. To be cared for is a basic human need.[54] To be in a caring relation with another human being is essential for the moral and psychological health of the community. Noddings has received some amount of criticism for her understanding of the limits of caring, and for the unequal power dynamics involved in caring. I believe what Noddings helps us understand are the very real dynamics of caring in the real world. She writes insightfully from personal experience:

> This attitude of warm acceptance and trust is important to all caring relationships. We are primarily interested in parent-child and teacher-student relationships but it is clear that caring is completed in all relationships through the apprehension of caring by the cared-for. When this attitude is missed, the one who is the object of care-taking feels like an object. He is being treated, handled by formula. When it is present and recognized, the natural effect of motivation is enhanced.[55]

In other words, both parties "are constrained by an ethic of care."[56]

Friendship emerges from the contexts of empathy and caring. Friendship is "a relation of mutuality, respect, fidelity, confidence, and affection."[57] Friendship focuses intentionally on community, honesty, non-exclusivity, flexibility, and other-directedness.[58] Friendship is an ethical practice of thoughtfulness.[59] Roberta C. Bondi talks about the ethical practice of friendship in term of power relations, concluding that "no human relationship can be described accurately as a friendship where one person is powerless and vulnerable while the other holds all the power, has no needs, and is invulnerable to hurt from the other"[60] Friendship is the relational pattern that guides all conversation with the stranger. It is the method, the hermeneutical process, of solidarity. Friendship is justice embodied.

This is not to imply that friends are always of a single mind. Within every friend is the stranger. A friend is not a perfect person, simply one who chooses to err on the side of friendship. Within the friend is the stranger, and this stranger manifests itself in different ways. C. G. Jung once asked the following question, "What if I should discover that the least amongst them all, the poorest of all the beggars, the most impudent of all the offenders...are within me...that I myself am the enemy who must be loved—what then?"[61]

Friendship is hard, deliberate work. Friendship is inner-directed, as well as outer-directed. It is not a means to perfection, nor an avenue to easy or absolute clarity about decision making in every situation. The art and act of friendship are a way of building communities of diversity. Being a friend is an act of hospitality because friendship implies a humane pattern of solidarity with all.

Empathy creates the space in which caring and friendship as ways of knowing may be practiced. Empathy, caring, and friendship are ways of knowing, ways of living interdependently in communities of difference. Together, they embody a process of radical dialogue in which transformation may take place. Empathy, caring, and friendship move beyond tolerance as a basic orientation of taking seriously the fact of increasing diversity, including religious diversity, in the world. Empathy, caring, and friendship are ways of knowing and radical ways of engaging in dialogue with the "other."

Empathy and Forgiveness

In my many interviews with adults about their experiences of childhood bullying, there is one constant. That one constant is that the adult who was bullied as a child will not forgive the bully. This is the most significant long-term effect for adults who have been bullied as children. But lack of forgiveness of the bully is not limited to events that occur in childhood. How many of us have been bullied as adults—and how many of us have wondered if we dare consider forgiveness? The issue of forgiveness is essential to consider in relation to violence, for if the violated person will not forgive the person who has brought humiliation, pain, and worse, the violated person's heart can become entrapped and deformed by the very corrosive violence from which she or he wishes to be released.

The lack of forgiveness is a sign of the very fatalism (hopelessness) that fills the heart by being terrorized by the bully—long after the bully has vanished physically. Very frequently, fatalism is the experience of bullied persons or groups. Fatalism is the assumption that things cannot change. Fatalism presumes that people cannot change. Fatalism is the assumption that one is powerless to affect change. Fatalism presumes that repentance and transformation are not possible. Personal change is not possible. Social change is not possible. The violence of force teaches us that there is not an I and a Thou, but an I and an It. The other person is not fully human. I am not fully human because I have enjoyed violent dependence, or because I could not care for myself alone.

Forgiveness does not mean to forget the violence that has taken place nor to minimize the consequences of violence. Forgiveness is a relational practice through which the I is restored and through which the Thou is restored. Forgiveness is a practice of empathy in which pride and dignity in self are restored, where movements toward reconciliation with self and others are begun. In March 2001, I was amazed by a news report about a group of Buddhists in Thailand who were meeting together as "The Good Deeds Club." This group of persons had organized a large prayer service "seeking forgiveness on behalf of the ruling Taliban group in Afghanistan that last month destroyed the statues of Buddha."[62] Official word from the group summarized the motivation for the prayer service. "We want to show the Taliban that although we were hurt by their actions, we forgive them and wish them happiness."[63] I was stunned by the action of these Buddhists, and I shared the story with friends at a meeting at Union Theological Seminary in New York a few days later. Our meeting included persons representing major religious groups in the United States. A sense of deep listening and introspection filled those with whom I spoke about this event. At the conclusion of the meeting, my spouse and I visited the Statue of Liberty—choosing to save a visit to the World Trade Center until our next visit to New York in November. Today, even more than in March 2001, the actions of the Buddhists in Thailand continue to draw me back to wonder about the meaning and expression of forgiveness in times such as these.

Forgiveness is a convers(at)ion between self, others, and God. It is a "conversion" because we are changed as the result of caring "conversation." This conversation of forgiveness takes place "at" or within a specific location or context, at a particular time. Today, ours is a context of political speeches about an Axis of Evil, about nuclear targeting of foes (as well as friends), about weapons of mass destruction, about collateral damage, and about some million troops lined on the Kashmiri border. Ours is a time and place where Iraq is full of armies and facing an uncertain future and where Israel and Palestine are embraced in a dance of death. Our "at" are broken schools where teachers are harmed emotionally and physically by enraged students and out-of-control parents. Conversion is always contextual and contextually relational. The convers(at)ion about the relation of bullying and forgiveness is concrete, earthy, and real.

The Meaning of Forgiveness

As I began writing this section of the book about forgiveness, my computer broke down. A technician came to my office, unscrewed about a dozen screws, unattached and reattached wires of many colors, took out a large metal piece that revealed electronic circuitry of the most amazing sorts, and replaced it with a new one. In less than fifteen minutes, the technician had restored the broken computer. In fact the technician said that the computer was now better than the original one that came off the assembly line.

Sometimes it is easy to equate the ease and timely repair of electronic gadgets with the process of forgiveness. Forgiveness is messy and takes a long time. We live in a culture and in an era when we have become accustomed to fast food, road rage, fast repairs, and even fast wars. If we have to wait more than two minutes for our microwave to cook something, we feel pressed for time and rushed. Pastoral theologian David W. Augsburger reminds us that human relationships are anything but products on a production line. He writes that "the bridges of human relationship are not easy to build; and once built, they are not simple to maintain; and if they endure, a costly toll is charged for each crossing."[64]

Forgiveness cannot and should not be rushed. Forgiveness is not the same as forgetting. Forgiveness is not pardon, nor is it a form of denial that yearns for a quick fix. Forgiveness is not something earned. Forgiveness is a conscious and thoughtful decision. Forgiveness, to paraphrase theologian Jon Sobrino, is to decide to act in a Christian way against sin.[65] To decide to act in a Christian way against sin is to risk, to be courageous, to be vulnerable. For often in the process of forgiving we discover our own complicities in sin, which we at first thought were to be found only in the person whom we chose to forgive. Forgiveness takes simple categorizations of bully and victim and often reveals deeper relational complexities than may have been first imagined. How surprised the entire world was to learn that Winnie Madikizela-Mandela established the MUFC (Mandela United Football Club) to kill, torture, burn, and assault her perceived enemies. Revenge that emerged from the violence of apartheid seemed so uncharacteristic of this person. The Truth and Reconciliation Commission in South Africa concluded that she was "accountable, politically and morally, for the gross violations of human rights committed by the MUFC."[66] At the hearing for Winnie Madikizela-Mandela, Bishop Storey testified before the Truth and Reconciliation Commission that "one of the tragedies of life...is it is possible to become like that which we hate most, and I have a feeling that this drama is an example of that."[67]

Certainly there are situations in which the sin of violence is less ambiguous, in which power relations and violation are more clear. In such cases, to speak of victim and bully is more appropriate. But often the relationships maintained between persons and groups are more complicated. More often than not, in the process of forgiving the other person or group of persons, we discover our place in the process of sin. We sometimes forget that our encounters with sin can change us, even if we are unaware of its corrosive effects. Loss of trust in one's judgment or intuition, isolation for the purpose of avoiding friends, irrational guilt and loss of self-respect and pride are very often the results of our encounters with violence—yet few of us realize that these were the products of our relations with bullies.

Practical theologian John Patton has suggested that forgiveness is the "rediscovery [of] who one is beyond the experience of injury and brokenness."[68] To de-form patterns of self and others that have been deformed through relational violence is one of the goals of forgiveness. The bully has disrupted our taken-for-granted worlds, what Beverly Flanigan has called a shattering of "the injured's bedrock assumptions about life."[69] Such questions as, "Can I care for myself?" or "Will I trust others?" or "Is there a future without violence?" or "Dare I risk loving another person?" are bedrock questions.

Forgiveness recognizes that we are, to use the words of religious educator Thomas Groome, "pilgrims in time."[70] In forgiveness, God offers to us in God's very self a pattern of relational life that is worthy of emulation. One does not go to God to ask forgiveness of sin. To ask God to forgive our patterns of relational violence misses the point of the meaning of the resurrection of Jesus. The point of the resurrection of Jesus is that God is with us in hope, even when God's absence seems imminent. God is with us in the mysterious presence of the Holy Spirit, luring us back to ourselves and back to others in relational patterns without violence. We are copartners with God in righteousness in a costly experiment of nonviolent relational living. Christians believe that such experimental living acts as a signal of healing to a very wounded, violent, revengeful, and frightened world.

In time (past, present, future) we forgive ourselves and others. Theologian Marjorie Suchocki correctly notes that forgiveness may be defined as "willing the well-being of those involved in violation."[71] Forgiveness understood in this way allows us to recognize that what has happened in the past need not continue into the present or future. By placing our memory of violation in the past, we may will the well-being of the other without being trapped by the patterns of sin in the past. Forgiveness may result in reconciliation, but often does not. Sometimes it is well to separate oneself from a bully, and reconciliation does not take place. Forgiveness is an act of justice and peace that need not include emotional resolution between persons and groups. Forgiveness is relational, but not always neat and tidy. It could very well be that if one has no voice in a context of bullying, and if nobody who witnesses the bullying is willing to become the voice of the abused person through advocacy, the best thing for the victim of violence to do is to remove herself or himself from the context of mindless violence. Often persons or groups do not know (nor can they recognize) that they are practicing violence. In these situations the victim of violence is considered to be a troublemaker, crazy, or just plain wrong. Removing oneself from such a context of violence can be an act of enormous risk and courage. To seek interpersonal reconciliation within the context of violence may not be possible, in such cases, without subjecting oneself to further violation. Where one has no voice, nor advocates to give voice for the voiceless, attempts at ongoing violation are probable. Sometimes the only way to claim human dignity is to leave the environment behind. Jesus recognized that sometimes people do not know what they are doing, yet Jesus taught us that forgiveness is still possible. Even in leaving situations for dignity and safety reasons, the Christian is not fatalistic. Hope is not the same as optimism. Hope (the opposite of fear) is grounded in the belief of the power of God's doxology. Optimism is more likely than not based on unrealistic and naïve assumptions about progress. Optimism has no place in the Christian life. Hope is central to the Christian life.

By saying that the violation should be placed in the past, am I suggesting that bullying be forgotten? No, that would be to misunderstand forgiveness. The cloth of our lives was shredded. That happened. To deny that the violation took place would be self-deceptive. We take our whole story, which may include bullying, with us along life's path. We cannot fix it. We cannot fix it, but we can begin the long process of remembering parts of ourselves shadowed or deleted by bullying. We can tell our stories by drawing on such negative funding events of life to negate hopelessness and fatalism. We can tell our stories afresh without getting stuck in the stagnant pools of revenge—pools from which the revenge-driven person or group drinks, aware or unaware.

Victims of violation carry that violation throughout all life. That violation is part of the person or group's story. But the event of violation is not the end of the story. Those who practice forgiveness are not entrapped by violence, but are transformed by love and by hope.

Christian religious educator Peter Gilmour has spent much time wondering about the ways people encounter God in the everyday world. Gilmour concludes:

> The interplay of memory, reflection, imagination, and expression creates sacred texts. These sacred texts, stories of reflected-upon life events, embody and express individual and social, personal, and communal significances. They reveal many things, but, most important, they reveal the transcendent dimensions of life. Things divine and the divine itself are made manifest through memoir. This does not happen through a grand synthesis of abstract theology or through an overwhelmingly charismatic hierophany, but in bits and pieces, in the shreds and shards of day-to-day experiences.[72]

The shreds and shards of our day-to-day experiences form memory that is grounded in hope. Often the victim of violence is called on to give voice to God's anguish in the world by telling her or his story of abuse. This takes enormous courage. This also takes enormous moral imagination. To break a cycle of violence is to participate in the work of God on earth. Forgiveness is both a gift and a decision. The bully is called on to repent—to turn around. This takes enormous courage. This also takes enormous moral imagination. To confess that an entire institution acted as a bully is an act of moral courage and imagination.

The document *Memory and Reconciliation: The Church and the Faults of the Past* was drafted by a committee of The International Theological Commission in Rome, and subsequently given permission for publication by Cardinal Ratzinger in December 1999. This document was a response to the Apostolic Letter *Tertio Millennio Adveniente*, published in 1994, in which John Paul II wrote, "Another painful chapter of history to which the sons and daughters of the Church must return with a spirit of repentance is that of the acquiescence given, especially in certain centuries, to *intolerance and even the use of violence* in the service of truth."[73]

For many in the Roman Catholic Church, this document was a scandal. John Paul II had asked for such a study, looking forward to the Great Jubilee of the Year 2000. John Paul II had particular interest in the relations between Jews and Christians through the centuries, a relation marred by Christian anti-Semitism. Among the commission document's opening words is the sentence, "in the entire history of the Church there are no precedents for requests for forgiveness by the Magisterium for past wrongs."[74] For many laity in the Catholic Church, trust of the Church was shaken. How can it be that the Church could ever be wrong? What can we believe? What are other religious traditions going to think of us?

In this decision, the Vatican demonstrated what I believe to be an imaginative and risky experiment in forgiveness. There is no way to pretend that the Church has not acted inappropriately toward others, particularly the Jews, in the past. Moving beyond boundaries of denial, the Pope in humility imagined what it might be like to break cycles of violence. To be sure, relations between Catholics and Jews and increasingly Catholics and Muslims have moved forward in positive ways—unimaginable only a decade ago.[75]

In August 2000, the Congregation for the Doctrine of Faith published the declaration *Dominus Iesus: On the Unicity and Salvific Universality of Jesus Christ and the Church.*[76] It is an odd document in the post-Vatican II era. By the title, one may discern that the document essentially says that all persons (not just Catholics) of the world must accept Jesus Christ in order to be saved.[77] Persons of many religious faiths, justifiably, responded with negative comment. Jewish persons in particular may have understood this document to be little more than another example of anti-Semitism. It seemed that in less than a year, the Church had extended its heart in seeking forgiveness, only in the end to take back its hope-filled words.

Church historians will have their day with both documents. But the importance of "Memory and Reconciliation" and "Dominus Iesus" for our discussion of violence and forgiveness is this: Patterns of domination and violence are very difficult to break. "Memory and Reconciliation" is a document of empathy and hospitality. "Dominus Iesus" is a document of fear, denigration, and bullying. It is the same in our own lives. In the process of forgiveness, we and those who have bullied us (or those whom we have bullied), will take two steps forward and one step back.[78] We should accept this, knowing that forgiveness does not and will not happen once and for all. The issue is not perfection, but direction with conscious intent. There are days when some of us will feel secure and self-confident, while other days we will be tempted to drink (and probably will drink) of the stagnant waters of revenge. The good news is that God is with us in this very messy and sloppy process, luring us to new imagination and to new life with ourselves and with those around us.

The Process of Forgiveness

As we forgive, and as we are forgiven by others, we discover the presence of God's doxological Spirit. L. Gregory Jones, dean of the Divinity School at Duke University, says that forgiveness is "offered as a gift to others so that the cycles [of violence] need not be repeated or exacerbated."[79] We have seen that forgiveness is also a gift to ourselves and to our communities. There is nothing linear about the process of forgiveness, no sequential steps that one may follow with care in order to know when forgiveness has taken place. But as we discover the power of a humanity that is forgiving and forgiven,[80] we can anticipate anger, denial, maybe even depression. We can anticipate memory and imagination to be in competition with each other sometimes, and in harmony at other times. We know that we need to understand our role in the act of violence, and we know that we need to become God's voice against violation. Sometimes, when we are unable to speak, we may need to have advocates speak God's word for us. We may feel ashamed. We may feel relieved. We may come to understand that our experience of violence is part of a web of violence that permeates the whole world. That is especially hard for many of us to encounter—especially for the first time. Inherited sin is something that a skilled counselor may help us see more clearly.[81] Sometimes talking with our friends will help. Sometimes talking to our pillows or our pets will help. Sometimes we will have a moment of insight after seeing a movie, reading a book, or observing the ways adults discipline children in the local shopping mall.

A person who practices forgiveness needs the support of a healthy community of faith. Forgiving and seeking to be forgiven are best accomplished in community with others. We need the support of the community not to turn away from the journey. We will notice from time to time that the community itself is re-formed because of our story, our bits and pieces of everyday life. As our lives begin to naturally model a compassionate confrontation with sin,[82] our joy in life will increase. Our participation in the doxology of God will become more and more the defining source of who we are.

In my view, the practice of forgiveness is a way of praying for ourselves, our neighbors, and our earth. Prayer is enabled by the Holy Spirit among us, through us. All true prayer is focused on restored relationships to self and others. All true prayer is inherently nonviolent. In this way, Christian life, forgiveness, nonviolence, and prayer form a seamless garment. As we forgive our trespasses and those who trespass against us, we will with God be partners in creating new life in the world.

Forgiveness and Children

You might be asking yourself the question, "While I understand what is being said about forgiveness from the perspective of an adult, how do these things apply to children who are being bullied?" This is a good question, one that deserves special attention.

Recall the story in chapter 1 of forgiveness in the life of Ruby Bridges. Recall the story in chapter 2 of the lack of forgiveness in the life of Karl. Recall also that empathy begins to develop in children by about eighteen months—maybe earlier. It has also been noted that the social support systems of the child, within and outside the family, are crucial to the pattern of development by the child. With these perspectives, let us begin our discussion.

It is my experience that children develop increasing capacity over time to reflect on experience. The younger the child, the more likely that the child reacts rather than reflects before action is taken. In time the child begins to reflect on life around her or him and develops the capacity for what educator and psychologist Robert Kegan calls "the capacity to take command of one's impulses (to have them, rather than be them)."[83] As time goes on, the child will become increasingly conversational and interpersonal. If life goes well, the child will be able to distinguish self from others. If life does not go well, the child will tend to lose self in the interpersonal context—unable to distinguish self from group. This has particular significance for the development of moral reasoning. If a child is unable to distinguish her or his own choices from the choices of the group, the child can end up following others—even if this proves to be dangerous or violent.

Within healthy and affirming social and family contexts, the child experiences from the earliest of years—even before the child is able to talk—patterns of caring, hospitality, friendship, and forgiveness—in the day-to-day life of relatedness. The way that parents handle disagreements and crises form the taken-for-granted environment of the child. When young siblings have conflict, the children are helped by adult caregivers to understand, even in early years, the place of consequences. Love and caring are expressed in the ways in which parents and children in a household respond to those times when forgiveness is required.

The story of Ruby Bridges comes to mind here. My students in seminary classes I teach about children inevitably ask the question, "Did Ruby really know what she was saying? Wasn't Ruby too young to understand the meaning of forgiveness?" These are good questions, but miss the mark. In a household where forgiveness is a basic Christian practice, Ruby enacted the values and caring of her household. In a real way, she was an ambassador of forgiveness, sent into the world by her family. At age six, could Ruby understand the process of forgiveness offered to those "who do not know what they do"? It appears to me that two things are going on with Ruby. First, she is developing as a wonderful human being—the result of a loving household where empathy is practiced. She knows who she is, and she is not taken up by the anger of the crowd. But something else is going on too. She uses the language and action of the household (which represents a safe and caring place where adults will protect her) to express her childhood faith and caring. Certainly, Ruby will continue to grow in faith throughout life. But she is modeling a mature faith that is congruent with her home environment (which includes her church environment) and with developmental capacities. Ruby responded to the bullying crowd as she did because she was supported by adults, had a clear and growing understanding of her own self, and took as her own the patterns of caring as practiced in her household.

With Karl, we have another kind of example. As I reflect on Karl's story, I am amazed by the "spark" of Karl's spirit that endured almost unbelievable testing. Karl did not feel safe at home or at school. His father modeled a pattern of relatedness that was both violent and judgmental. In horror, we read how Karl's father responded to the tattoo. Karl, seeking to avoid punishment, used a Brillo pad to avoid pain and shame. As the bullying developed over time, there were no support systems at home or in his larger social context. He did not feel safe, because he was not safe. There were no adults to protect him. He internalized his anger. The pressure of this internalization finally burst. He distinguished himself from others through anger and violence—yet continued to desire to be part of the group. This double bind, wanting to belong but not belonging, gave rise to revenge, not forgiveness. In the end, he was out of control and alone. While in Vietnam, the thought of the bullies at the prom—a place Karl very much wanted to be—was almost too much to bear.

If as adults we do not provide an adequate environment for the practice of forgiveness, children will not be able to invent such an environment or set of practices on their own. If as adults we do not take seriously the significance of peer violence in the lives of our children, we are playing roulette with their safety and well-being and with their future spiritual development. It is true that each child has her or his own personality and that some children are "easier" than others. I love working with first- and second-grade children, and it amazes me to see the strong personalities already in process at ages six and seven! But no child is predestined to be a bully, and no child is predestined to be a victim of bullying. The way empathy is practiced in the home, and particularly the way forgiveness is enacted by significant adults in the home, is crucial to the healthy development of the child—and her or his ability to distinguish self from group in ways that are based on caring, not on ways that require the violence of revenge.

Summary: Bullying as Spiritual Crisis

What does it mean to say that bullying is a spiritual crisis? A Christian spirituality focuses on the ways in which a person relates with others, with self, with God, and with the earth. Spirituality that is Christian is basically a holistic way of viewing the human person in her or his wide range of relationships. A Christian spirituality that is doxological brings the praise of God to all contexts where persons are in relation with others. Bullying gives form to sin in the whole field of human relationships. Bullying affects a person's relation with others, self, God, and the earth.

Bullying is the violation of life-giving interdependence, and therefore of relational personhood as revealed to us by God through Jesus Christ and the Spirit. As a process of violation of personhood, violence is the chosen (even if unconscious) means of corruption of God's gift of human being and human becoming. The interdependence of bully and bullied models a relation that is both sinful and destructive. Bullying is the negation of the praise of God. It distorts the relational process of God with and for human beings, interdependence, to violate the other person.

The lure by God of persons to Godself and to one another within a cultural context that extols a myth of tolerance is an odd and potentially dangerous combination. Diversity is not something the bully can accept. The bully can seek to be in relation with others, but only by negating their differences. This negation of difference may be through ongoing emotional abuse, physical violence, or even elimination of others. To merely tolerate others who are different is to turn others into objects or things. Peace might be maintained by minimizing opportunity for radical dialogue between persons and groups who are different from one another. But this is an inadequate and uneasy peace, one that breeds stereotypes and worse.

When the enforcing mechanisms of tolerance are broken down, the fruits of tolerance are revealed through subsequent acts of random brutality. The Christian practice of empathy provides a powerful and hopeful alternative to tolerance. Empathy presumes diversity, hospitality, and the practice of friendship. The opposite of intolerance is not tolerance. The opposite of intolerance is empathy. Empathy appears to be at the very heart of who God is for us. Practicing the presence of God means to practice empathy, entering into the suffering of the other brother and sister.

Within a cultural context of toleration, where separation and stereotype are virtually inevitable, fatalism, fear, distrust, entitlement, and envy tell us that forgiveness is not possible—or that forgiveness is a sign of weakness. A life grounded in the partnership of empathy, hospitality, and friendship, on the other hand, is a life of hope. It is possible that one cannot experience hope without experiencing first despair. But hope is the negation of fear and fatalism. Hope insists that change is possible. Change is a relational, transformational process that requires empathy as a way of knowing. Without empathy, there can be no forgiveness, no healing, and therefore no experience of the human self in relation with the human others. Forgiveness is a sign of Christian hope that God is ushering in a world of justice and harmony through our simple, daily relationships.

Chapter 4 describes some concrete ways the practices of empathy, hospitality, friendship, caring, and forgiving may be worked out in such contexts as school, home, church, and work.

CHAPTER 4

Ways of Practicing Empathy

In this chapter, I explore four different ways of practicing empathy: (1) writing a bully policy for your church or school; (2) taking virtues to school; (3) making critical literacy a habitual Christian practice; and (4) taking an inventory of the practices of empathy in worship. Each of these can be used in at least three ways. You may find these ways of practicing empathy valuable in your own devotional time and reflection. In addition, each of the four concrete ways of practicing empathy may be used for a formal one-hour study for your church's teacher education program, or for use as the basis of an educational workshop in a retreat setting. Finally, you may find that these four topics provide the basis for conversation in a Sunday adult education setting. There are many ways of practicing empathy, but I have found that these four approaches come up again and again as I talk with adult groups in local congregational settings. So let's begin by learning how to write a bully policy for your church or school.

Writing a Bully Policy for Your Church or School

Bullying can and does take place in the church or in the church-related school. Many churches and church-related schools are beginning to consider the importance of an institutional bully policy. Why is it important to consider a bully policy? A bully policy (1) defines what bullying is, (2) gives public voice to the consequences of bullying, (3) acts as an important teacher education document, and (4) describes methods of intervention that may be useful in helping both the bully and the victim of bullying.

In many religious institutional settings, administrators and teachers have no clear idea about what constitutes bullying. Before bullying can be prevented, administrators and teachers need a definition of bullying. Parents, administrators, and teachers must be aware of the consequences of bullying. To define what bullying is without clearly delineating the consequences of bullying is of little value to anyone. Who shall report bullying? To whom shall the report be made? What, then, shall we do? These are important questions to address in any bully policy.

A bully policy can also become an important part of teacher orientation or teacher training. Most teachers with whom I am acquainted agree that addressing violence in the schools is crucial. They want to stop bullying in their classrooms, cafeterias, buses, libraries, and playgrounds. But I find that these teachers only rarely know what bullying is, how they may stop bullying, or to whom they should report bullying. It is an ethical imperative to give administrators, parents, students, and teachers helpful guidance and support.

Ken Rigby, an Australian scholar on bullying has discovered that in many schools an ethos or culture of violence is accepted as normal. He calls this situation "institutionalized bullying."[1] This is more frequent than we would like to think. As I visit churches and schools, it is not uncommon to have a discussion of bullying challenged by teachers, parents, and administrators with such comments as, "Ron, certainly you know that boys will be boys." Or I have been told, "Ron, don't worry about bullying. Kids are just being kids." Teachers and administrators in such settings who are in charge of the educational ethos choose to ignore bullying— and by so doing, allow (and perpetuate) its presence.

Rigby gives an example of a bullying policy from Xavier College, a boys school in Melbourne, in his book, *Bullying in Schools: And What to Do About It.*[2] The following example of a bullying policy for your religious school or religious education program is based in part on the Xavier College model described by Rigby. As you seek to write a bullying policy for your own educational setting, the major headings of the policy below may prove to be practical and useful. Specific issues that arise from your educational context will necessarily modify and enrich the bully policy suggested. Be sure to pass your bully policy by your teachers, parents, and legal counsel before implementing it on a school, district, or program-wide basis.

A Sample School Bully Policy

At *(fill in the name of your school here)* School, there is zero tolerance of bullying. Teachers, administrators, children, and parents are committed to a schooling environment in which mutual respect, caring, friendship, forgiveness, and hospitality are practiced. We do not believe that bullying is an inevitable part of childhood. We believe that children learn best in a nonviolent community.

Bullying Defined

Bullying is a behavioral manifestation of spiritual crisis in which an individual bully or group of bullies seeks relation with another person or persons through repeated acts of violence over time. The behaviors of bullying are intended to hurt and disturb others. These acts of violence may be physical and/or emotional (threatened or carried out). There is always an imbalance of power between the bully and the bullied. Bullying can take place by individuals, informal groups of persons, formal organizations, or nations.

The following are bullying behaviors:

- Belittling others because of religious traditions
- Belittling others because of race and/or cultural identities
- Belittling others because of pattern of speech
- Belittling others because of physical appearance
- Belittling others because of an emotional, mental, or physical disability
- Belittling others because of sexual orientation
- Hitting, slapping, or pushing persons over time
- Starting and/or perpetuating rumors, making suggestive or derogatory sexual comments, or making bodily gestures that intimidate or embarrass others
- Shunning and/or silencing others
- Demanding money, personal belongings, and sexual favors by extortion
- Making emotional threats, including name-calling and "dissing"

If We Are Victims of Bullying,

- We may feel unsafe and afraid, with little hope that life will ever change.
- We may be too embarrassed to talk with parents or teachers about the situation.
- We may feel humiliated and enraged.
- Our school grades may get worse.
- We may have low self-concept.
- We may withdraw from social functions, such as dances, parties, and youth groups.
- We may lose interest in church, prayer, and community service.
- We may become very negative at home, treating parents and siblings poorly.
- We may erupt in acts of violence ourselves in order to protect ourselves (because of feelings of frustration or hopelessness).
- We may become self-destructive in our behavior.
- We are created in the image of God.

If We Are the Bully,

- We may have been bullied at home by adults and/or siblings. We may have been bullied at school by teachers, administrators, or bus drivers.
- We may appear to be popular. Or we may have a small circle of friends who are not in the "mainstream" of the school.
- We may make cloaked threats, such as, "After school tonight!"
- We may be con artists, appearing to be "good" around adults, but being violent around other children.
- We may have low self-concept.
- We may know no other way to be in relation with others than through the practices of bullying and violence.
- We may seek pleasure through violence.
- We may be older and bigger than those whom we bully.
- We are created in the image of God.

What Shall We Do Together to Prevent Bullying?

- Bullying is an issue for the entire school community: administration, teachers, staff, volunteers, parents, and students.

- The entire school community will model hospitality, caring, and friendship in word and action.

- The entire school community will refuse to be a bystander to bullying. Incidents or suspected incidents will be reported immediately to the appropriate Community Life Committee chairperson. This chairperson will be elected to serve a two-year term. The chairperson will be elected from the administration, teachers, and staff. The Community Life Committee will be composed of two persons elected annually from each of the following areas: administration, teachers, other staff, children (aged ten and above), parents, and other volunteers. The principal is a permanent member of this committee.

- The Community Life Committee will conduct an annual inservice day for administration, teachers, staff, and volunteers on the topic of bullying.

- The Community Life Committee will be committed to the value of diversity.

- Each member of the Community Life Committee will be on the lookout for spontaneous "acts of kindness." These acts of kindness will be publicized (by newsletter, electronic campus communication system, or other appropriate means) weekly. This will include all members of the school community.

- The Community Life Committee will act as a resource to the school for resources related to bullying.

- Each member of the Community Life Committee will be introduced to each class of students, to parents, and to staff. Each member will wear a special "CLC" button that everyone at school recognizes.

- The Community Life Committee will develop a system of procedures to be followed should an incidence of bullying arise.

What Shall Teachers Do to Prevent Bullying?

- Teachers will not ignore bullying behavior.

- Teachers will intervene, even at risk to personal safety.

- Teachers will be on time to class and to other school functions.

- Teachers will engage students in conversation about bullying.

- Teachers will take appropriate steps to stop bullying, including contacting the Community Life Committee.

- Lessons about respect for self and others will be part of an ongoing, integrated curriculum.

What Shall Students Do to Prevent Bullying?

- Students will recognize what bullying is.
- Students will not bully others, even if their best friends are bullying someone.
- Students will report bullying to a teacher, their parents, or a member of the Community Life Committee.
- If you are bullied or if you are the bully, take responsibility to talk with someone on the Community Life Committee.

What Can Parents Do to Prevent Bullying?

- Practice empathy at home.
- If your child talks to you about bullying, take her or him seriously. Contact the school immediately, referring to the bullying policy.
- Be familiar with the school's bullying policy.
- If your child is the bully, seek the school's help.
- If your child is bullied, do not encourage your child to seek revenge.
- If your child's grades fall significantly, if your child develops a pattern of sadness or despair, or if your child refuses to go to school, contact the school principal.
- Monitor playmates and know the families of your child's friends.
- If your child frequently complains of stomachaches or other illnesses, schedule a conference with your child's teacher.
- Tell your child that it is your responsibility as a parent to protect her or him and that parental involvement in matters of bullying is normal.
- Monitor television programs, video games, magazines, movies, and Internet sites that a child may access.

This kind of school policy should be posted on bulletin boards near the office of the principal (or director of religious education, headmaster or headmistress, dean, etc.). It should be displayed in places that children may feel unsafe (often locations that are less supervised or less structured), such as in bathrooms or on doorways leading to the playground. It should be a part of all handbooks, including the staff, volunteer, parent, and student handbooks. Parents should understand that bullying is not allowed in the school and that a zero-tolerance approach means that bullying results in consequences. I believe that it is important to have children serve on the Community Life Committee. While there are some confidential issues that would naturally require review by adults only, the child's experience of serving on such a committee can be positive and formative.

What about a procedural guide, once a case of bullying has been reported to the Community Life Committee? Creating a procedural guide will need to be among the first tasks of the Community Life Committee. Since each school will have different administrative structures and different understandings of discipline, it is not possible to generalize a process guide here. But whatever the specific process of discipline, there must be an attempt to intervene on the bully's behalf, as well as on the victim's behalf.

To suspend a bully for two days, for example, is punitive but rarely effective. The parents of the bully may profit by taking parenting classes required by the school. The bully may profit by being assigned a teacher mentor. The bully may profit by becoming part of a group counseling process where identified bullies meet together under the care of a qualified therapist. This is not to say that suspension is inappropriate. Properly supervised, suspension is most appropriate.

But the bully is a part of a wider familial and social system that also needs to be addressed. The school ought not be surprised if the bully does not reform overnight. By the time the school receives a child, even a kindergarten child, the child's character has already been formed by significant adults and peers. Sometimes the damage done to the child's spirit is so deep that long-term professional care is the most appropriate intervention. If a school accepts a child as a student, it is the school's responsibility to minister to the whole child (including the family system), even if that child is a bully. There may come the pain-filled time when all attempts at intervention fail and the student must be asked to leave the school permanently. This is a choice only of last resort.

Similarly, if a child in your care has been the victim of bullying, it is likely that the child needs more care than simply removing the bully—*or removing the child from the situation*. Again and again I have seen parents who do not want to deal with the reasons why their child is a victim of bullying simply transfer their child to another school—in hopes that the child will be bullied no longer. Frequently, this results from the parent's need to understand the child as a victim unable to protect himself or herself. Children pick up on this implicit message and begin to believe that they cannot take care of themselves. Certainly, parents do not wish for their child to be bullied. But parents who do not look at their child's behavior in bully situations (by moving too quickly to blaming the bully for all the problems) may well find that the child is bullied again in the new school.

It is important to remember that the child's safety from abuse is essential. A child who is being victimized by a bully needs to know the ways in which the school will protect the child. Individual skills for coping with bullies may be suggested by caring adults: walking in groups with other children, avoiding a bully when possible, ignoring the negative comments of a bully, and saying "Quit it!" to the bully. Role play is valuable. These coping skills are important in order to remove oneself immediately from the bully. At the same time, such skills must not be understood as ends in themselves. Caring adults must take time and responsibility to ask the more long-term question, "Why is this child bullied again and again, regardless of school?" Seeking competent help for the child and her or his family may be the most caring thing for the adult to do for the child. Both short-term and long-term strategies must be considered for the bullied child.

Intimidation and humiliation cut deep into the soul of a child or of a young person. It is true that some children are bullied more than others. A child's introversion, sense of self, and possible lack of appropriate social skills are issues for the child's whole family— not just the child. Again, parenting classes for the family, counseling by a qualified therapist, teacher mentors, or socialization into school clubs help those involved begin to see the child as a whole person, not simply as the target of another person's aggression. Issues related to a school's recommendation of therapy for a child must be reviewed in terms of current law.

It is my experience that many parents can become agitated and hostile if it is suggested that their child has engaged in bullying behavior. Similarly, parents may become defensive and hostile if it is suggested that something about their child may invite bullying. Fortunately, this is not the case with the majority of parents, who seek the very best for their children. But sometimes the expectations that parents have for their child are so unrealistic and so high that they are unable to distinguish the difference between the behavior of the child and their own behavior. When adults feel that we are attacking them by bringing their child's behavioral pattern to light, we must be patient and practice active listening and active caring.

I have found this to be particularly true in a Sunday morning religious education program, where many parents seem to feel that Sunday school or catechetical instruction is a place where rules of behavior of weekday school do not apply. Many parents treat

Sunday morning religious education as a way to escape the reality of schooling during the week. One can understand the exhaustion of parents who have challenging children, and how an "escape" for a couple of hours on Sunday morning might be tempting. But the behavior of children on Sunday morning (or Sunday evening, Wednesday evening, etc.) should not be viewed as a free-for-all. Standards for conduct remain constant the whole week long.

Sometimes we have minimal standards for teachers of our children on Sunday mornings. As parents, we must advocate for quality standards of teacher education and training, even for short programs on Sunday mornings. Children must associate the church with safety from their earliest years. Children must not associate the church with lack of safety and chaos. For it is from the practices of life in the church that children learn those ways of life that are appropriate for the people of God. Nowhere in the life of the local church or parish can we learn the relational practices of Christian life more concretely or more powerfully than in worship.

Taking Virtues to School

There is a renewed attention today to character education and values in public schools. Some leaders in character education for public schools insist that there are basic human values that "transcend religious and cultural differences and express our common humanity."[3]

It has been the argument of this book that we are created by and for God and that God never ceases to draw humanity to Godself. Further, God invites humanity to a life of doxology (the praise of God) that is life-giving and full of hope. I would contend that all positive human values are gifts from God. We have a common humanity only because we are all created in the image of God. Rather than transcending religious and cultural differences, all positive values arise from humankind's concrete experiences of and responses to God. It is the specificity of values that differ from cultural group to cultural group that puts us face-to-face with our diversity.[4] Assuming that different cultural groups have different values, the goal is not to create some sort of universally applicable list of virtues that will apply to all people everywhere. Rather, the goal is to listen actively to one another in our diversity.

Traditional Christian Virtues

One religious community that has given much attention to the issue of virtues is the Christian community. A traditional Christian understanding of values distinguishes between cardinal virtues, theological virtues, gifts of the Holy Spirit, and fruits of the Holy Spirit. Before we suggest how these virtues might become part of the school, let us review briefly how these Christian virtues have been understood over time.

Saint Gregory of Nyssa, writing in the fourth century of the Common Era, concluded, "the end of the life of virtue is to become like God."[5] This is not a statement of idolatry, but a statement of Christian discipleship. Gregory goes on to suggest that as one hungers after any one virtue, she or he is partaking in all virtues, "for any one form of virtue, divorced from the others, could never by itself be a perfect virtue."[6] The Christian virtues are interdependent, giving depth and understanding in the midst of one another, not isolated nor independent. The traditional Christian "cardinal" virtues include prudence, temperance, fortitude, and justice. These virtues develop over time by practice, through education, and through choice. A prudent person is one who can make sound decisions based on Christian principles. A person of temperance is known for her or his moderation. A just person embodies a Christian understanding of God and neighbor, and is one who works for the common good. A person of fortitude is a person of moral conviction and moral strength.[7]

Cardinal Virtues and the Christian Life

What gives the cardinal virtues a particularly Christian focus? After all, persons outside Christianity could very well practice the cardinal virtues as outlined above. The theological virtues give the cardinal virtues their Christian focus. The theological virtues are faith, hope, and charity. Faith, hope, and charity are gifts from God that act as a foundation for all moral action. We are able to love God above all things and others as ourselves only because of the work of the Holy Spirit. The same could be said about faith and hope. To live in a way that connects faith and life, or to engage hope instead of fatalism is not a matter of the will alone, but a testimony to the presence of the Holy Spirit.

The fruits of the moral life given shape and form by the Holy Spirit are joy, peace, patience, gentleness, modesty, self-control, kindness, goodness, and generosity. Where there is no kindness or generosity, it is likely that the gifts of the Holy Spirit are not guiding and informing the cardinal virtues. The moral life is sustained by dispositions, again given as gifts to us by the Holy Spirit: wisdom, understanding, counsel, fortitude, knowledge, piety, and humble respect of God. Wisdom is not merely to be understood as something humans create on their own, but as something given to us by God—and something that draws us closer to God.[8]

Now we are ready to talk about the relation of the Christian school and virtues. The practice of virtues in a Christian school is not intended to make children into "good boys and good girls." The practice of virtues in a Christian school is not intended to make children more patriotic. The practice of Christian virtues in a Christian school is an essential way of acknowledging a pattern of attitudes and practices that focus on our love for God and on our love for our neighbors as ourselves—the practice of empathy. The practice of Christian virtues is fundamentally the practice of God's doxology for us, and as such is caring and nonviolent.[9]

From the earliest school experiences of a Christian child, it is completely appropriate to emphasize the cardinal virtues. It is equally important that adults understand the relation of ethical behavior and the Christian virtues. Within the framework in which Christians understand the cardinal virtues (the framework of theological virtues and the gifts/fruits of the Holy Spirit) a specific form of reflection and action is invited that seeks to take the good news of God's doxology seriously.

Virtues in Christian Education

I worry that many of our mainline Protestant and Catholic churches have forgotten about a Christian understanding of virtue. Two years ago, while teaching a graduate course entitled, "The Moral Lives of Children," I came to a point in the class when I asked my Christian students (all preparing for ordained ministry) where they had learned the basic values that guide their lives. Most of the students were in their late twenties. I expected students to say that they had learned values for a moral life from family, from church, or from significant Christian role models. The overwhelming answer from my students was quite different from what I had expected! The answer was, "What I have learned about the moral life came from Sesame Street." I was taken aback until I listened to what my students had to say.

On Sesame Street, my students were introduced to the importance of caring for everyone, regardless of gender, race, or economic class. My students learned how to solve situations of conflict. They learned how to act in public places, how to say "please" and "thank you," how to speak politely on the telephone, and how to invite persons of various disabilities to become part of the group. They learned how to respond appropriately to the death of older adults and how to celebrate interracial marriage. I pressed the point: "You cannot think of times in religious education programs or Christian school when you learned moral behaviors?" The overwhelming response was, "No." Students indicated that the content of the Christian faith had been good, but that practical and everyday life issues—moral issues—were not addressed, because there was no time in class to do so.

We have said that worship may be understood as a context for practicing empathy—but we have to help persons see with "new eyes" how this can be so. So also with the formation of character— we need to help persons see with "new eyes" how the cardinal virtues are an essential part of the presence and work of the Holy Spirit.

Again, it is completely appropriate for the parish school, Sunday school, catechesis programs, and other educational settings to focus on the cardinal virtues. Posters on classrooms and hallways with the cardinal and theological virtues, incorporation of values into the whole curriculum of the school, focus on virtues in the school's mission statement, and special assembly programs on virtues are completely appropriate. But lest the Christian school fall into mere moralism, the virtues must be understood as avenues through which the distinctive qualities of the Christian life may be understood—and through which God may be encountered.[10]

Can Virtue Be Taught?

A question that I am asked frequently is whether morals can be taught or not. My answer is that the moral life can be taught through modeling and through reflection on actions and decisions—within specific contexts. What do I mean by "within specific contexts"? A teacher is responsible for the behavior in her or his classroom. As early as kindergarten, a teacher can enter into conversation with students at the beginning of the school year about the kind of behavior that is acceptable and unacceptable in the classroom. Many younger students can understand the importance of rules for classroom behavior. These rules of conduct can be posted in the classroom and referred to and modified throughout the school year.

Beginning with clarity about those rules of conduct that provide for the safety of teachers and students may, in time, give rise to other conversations. Many children, for example, by age seven, are able to read (or understand when read to them) E. B. White's book *The Trumpet of the Swan*.[11] The moral dilemma that arises in the book (is stealing appropriate under these circumstances?) helps children to begin to develop a desire to ask, "How do I choose what is good or right?"[12] Early understandings of liberation may arise, particularly in terms of issues of fairness. By about age ten or eleven, many children are able to begin to interpret White's moral dilemmas in terms of their own life stories, and in terms of others who take very different perspectives. Moral dilemmas arising from literature (and other arts), life in school, life with peers, and life in church may be understood as "persistent life situations."[13] That is, the same or similar moral dilemmas will be revisited, reinterpreted, and debated again and again over a lifetime.

While a teacher can be responsible for the behavior of his or her community of learning in a specific classroom, the teacher cannot presume that the ethical practices of the classroom will necessarily transfer automatically to other places in the child's life. Each context of the child's life contains different relational patterns. Sometimes ethical behavior transfers to other areas (particularly if these contexts are similar to one another), but most times it does not. *The appropriate practice of the Christian life in the classroom may not transfer to other contexts, yet the classroom is a place of safety, caring, hospitality, and friendship while students are together.* When the ethos of the entire school is reflected in the practice of teaching and learning in the classroom, the school itself becomes a safe place in which the Christian virtues may be practiced. Where the values of the home reinforce the values of the school (and vice versa), transfer of learning between school and home is more likely to occur. But again, the values at work in the context of the school may not transfer easily to the other locations of the child's life (such as home, church, and leisure contexts).

In many Sunday catechetical programs and Sunday school programs, the issue of class rules and ethical behavior becomes problematic because children are increasingly sporadic in their attendance. The formation of a community of learning is difficult in these circumstances. Where there is a high turnover of students from week to week, teachers may need to begin each class session with the review of a single classroom rule. A class newsletter that can be taken home by children should contain the rules of classroom behavior. There are no easy answers here, but teaching cannot take place in a context without structure. Appropriate structure gives the student the sense of security needed to take risks in creativity. The more chaotic the ethos of a classroom, the less students will tend to risk thinking in new ways.

Virtues as Doxology

The values at work within a schooling context may encourage the practice of doxology. Values form an affective appreciation for a way of living, thinking, and acting. We know from the writing of such persons in the history of the Christian church as Saint Gregory of Nyssa that discussion about the relation of virtue and Christian life has taken place for centuries in the church ecumenical. While the cardinal virtues might be used by those inside or outside the church, what is distinctive about a Christian understanding of cardinal virtues is the virtues' relation to theological virtues and the gifts of the Holy Spirit. These virtues, when practiced within the context of a community such as a classroom, provide a structure for relationships between persons that invites critical reflection and interpretation of doxology in faith and life. Virtues are not to be viewed as educational goals so much as accepted values essential for the Christian formation of communal life. By reflecting deliberately on the virtues in the context of a school, teachers and students are renewing their commitment to a particular cultural order, one in which caring, friendship, and hospitality are hallmarks of life together. Virtues, interpretation of the meaning of life in context, and learning how to make choices are essential for persons of all ages who seek to "become like God"—partners with God's doxological work in the world.[14]

Critical Literacy

Theologian Catherine Mowry LaCugna defined doxology, we recall from chapter 1, as the praise of God. She encouraged us to think about doxology as a way of "actively resisting injustice, prejudice, and hatred."[15] LaCugna provides wonderful categories to help us to begin thinking about the ways we approach reading materials and other media in the home. The active Christian life is one of mindfulness and what we are calling here "critical literacy." The word *critical* does not mean grouchy or condemning. As used here, it means to be constructively mindful. We reflect, we interpret, and we evaluate things around us rather than pretending we are neutral or passive sponges that can and should soak up everything around us. "Critical literacy" is related to mindfulness. Critical literacy points to the careful evaluation of the inherent values of literature and media in order to raise consciousness of the distinction (or similarities) between doxology and what is being watched or read.

1. Evaluate What Is Around You. Let us explore a simple example as we begin. We have said that for LaCugna, doxology implies the themes of actively rejecting injustice, prejudice, and hatred. We have suggested that the practices of doxology are practices of empathy, friendship, hospitality, and caring. What if we applied these simple criteria to a recent sports magazine that appeared at my teenage son's door? Every year, this magazine has a special issue of bikini-clad women. This swimsuit edition of this popular magazine has great appeal to teenage boys. Nearly all his friends at his Christian high school have seen a copy of the magazine. As a Christian adult who cares for this child, what shall I do?

Sitting down with children and reading the books and magazines they are reading, or talking about Web sites they have visited is completely appropriate. Does the portrayal of women in this magazine help us engage in doxology, the praise of God? When women are portrayed in ads with a liquor bottle next to them, what is being communicated? When the heads of women are cut off in the picture, only to show other parts of the anatomy, are we encouraging friendship—or are we turning the women into objects for use? How does it make women feel who do not have perfect bodies to see men reading such magazines? Do men develop feelings of caring and hospitality for themselves, others, and the earth as a result of reading the sports magazine?

Popular culture is so unconscious of its violence against women through the distribution of such magazines that it is unlikely that an average teenage boy would see anything wrong with them. Choices for doxology are very often choices to exclude some things from our time and experience. The cardinal virtue of temperance comes with a significant cost in our culture, where almost anything goes and where so much is available so readily.

2. Being Mindful Is a Christian Choice. I can imagine that some of the readers of this book may be mumbling, "But if I have to be mindful about everything I read or watch, I will be exhausted by the end of the day. All I want to do after a day of school or work is to sit down and watch television and not think at all." This is a good point. People are working a lot in our culture, and most people are very tired by the end of a workday. But there are many other ways of relaxing, of taking time to rest, than putting one's mind (and one's morals) in neutral. The habitual patterns of relaxation we have learned through the years are hard to break, but not impossible to break if we choose to do so. Sometimes being a Christian is a countercultural activity, and in an entertainment saturated culture it is more likely to be countercultural than not. The critical literacy exercise that I have suggested in regard to a sports magazine may be applied similarly to television programs, movies, Web sites, comic books, and video games.

A local mall here in Atlanta has a very popular video arcade. Children and parents visit the arcade all the time. I have been amazed by the many games, increasingly stunning in their electronic sophistication and increasingly realistic images, that include bloodshed and violence. Bloodied body parts are blown off, heads and legs are shot with bullets, and keen attention is needed to complete the game. One such video game requires the player to hold an electronic device shaped like a handgun in order to kill intruders, which then produces a feeling of success by the scoring of points. Children (and I suspect many adults as well) learn to be experts in a variety of lethal weapons and methods of destruction. The current wave of "militainment," the intentional blending by filmmakers and video game producers of entertainment and military weaponry/combat scenarios (exemplified by the horrific movie *The Sum of All Fears*[16]), extends the boundary-blending of reality and violence even more by connecting implicitly violence and patriotism. In other words, the desired outcome of these militainment products is for the consumer to be prepared at all times and in all places for violence, with that violence providing opportunities for patriotic heroism. The paranoia of being on guard at all times and in all places is a fruitful ground for fear and the inevitability of violence to take root— further desensitizing us while simultaneously glamorizing the need for violence.

3. Consider the Ways Children Understand. Children younger than five (sometimes extending into the second grade) often do not have the developmental ability to discern between pretend and real. Nor is the younger child's ability to think about time the same as an adult's. This is hard for many adults to understand. The repeated television play of the attack on the World Trade Center in New York may help to clarify this developmental issue. As an adult watched television coverage of the attack on the World Trade Center, deep emotions were stirred. Yet the adult was able to discern that a replay of the planes crashing into the towers was a replay. Younger children do not have the ability to think chronologically as adults do. Every time the plane attack was replayed, the younger child thought it was the first time.

Moreover, the line between fantasy and reality is blurred for the younger child. Younger children can experience intense video games as real. This sometimes happens for older children and teenagers as well. Younger children learn that if a combatant's head is blown off, in moments it will be restored completely. It is not a matter of believing that one's violent acts on another have consequences—the person blown apart simply comes back to life. I have found in my own work with children in the first and second grades that they are amazed when stabbing another child with a pencil, hitting another child with a lunchbox, or hitting another child with a piece of wood actually hurts the other child. It does not occur to many impressionable children that violence causes pain for those who are violated. Don't get me wrong. There are many good educational video games for children. But children ought not be exposed to those video games that present violence. When children (and adults) begin to associate violence with pleasure and pride of accomplishment, the human spirit is diminished. For caregivers to allow younger children to play violent video games is a form of child abuse. The same would be true for taking a child to a "R" rated horror show or a movie with graphic violence and sex. The adult who is a child advocate chooses to remove children from such contexts.

4. *Education as Entertainment.* As a religious educator, it is my conviction that children are overstimulated in our culture. Some educators are advocating "edu-tainment" in the classroom to keep up with the child whose attention span is short, and for whom learning and frenetic behavior are synonymous. This is not a time for adults in the school, home, or church to adapt educational programming to cultural dysfunction. Children need to experience calm, quiet, and the joy of reading a book far more than they need to become proficient consumers of entertaining violence and overstimulation. This is true for adults as well, but it is particularly essential for young children.

Critical Literacy as Doxology

Critical literacy is not a form of cultural prudishness, nor is it a way of taking fun away from children. Critical literacy is an invitation to take seriously the style of life required by doxology. In our day and times, this may well be the most important—and the most difficult—discipline for those who care about and care for our children.

Taking an Inventory of Practices of Empathy in Worship

About a year ago, a major news organization learned that I had interest in the topic of bullying. News cameras came to the seminary where I was teaching, and a particularly insightful news reporter interviewed me. Afterward the cameraman engaged me in a long conversation about his approach to parenting and about how important this issue is for our society today. A week later an editor from the news organization contacted me and said that while the interview looked good, I did not promote resources that a television watcher could go out and purchase on the topic of bullying as a spiritual crisis. I told the editor that I was working on a book, but she wanted something concrete that could be purchased. I said that the primary public places that children, young people, and adults may practice empathy were in the local parish, church, synagogue, mosque, or temple. It was there, I suggested, that persons of many different religions seek to shape their lives in ways that reflect their deepest beliefs about God, other persons, and the earth. The editor wanted nothing of this! The editor wanted a quick fix, something that was packaged and readily available to the consumer public. The news story was pulled, never to be aired.

This is not a story about sour grapes. It is an illustration of how often in our culture, including in our communities of faith, we ignore the life of the local religious community as *the* central place for practicing empathy through acts of hospitality, caring, and friendship. It almost never occurs to most of us that Christian worship is a place where we practice a way of empathetic life. We all know that it is true that some religious communities practice intolerance, violence, and hate. But I contend that most religious communities throughout the world seek peace and justice in ways that invite persons into a way of practicing faith that is full of life and hope. In my view, our religious communities are one of the very few places left in our culture where groups of persons may practice empathy *intentionally.* In our quick-fix, individualistic, self-help culture, communities of faith that attend to the doxological life over time are many times forgotten or overlooked. In the words of Don E. Saliers, F. N. Parker Professor of Theology and Worship at Candler School of Theology in Atlanta, Georgia, "Questions concerning Christian ethics and the shape of the moral life cannot be adequately understood apart from thinking about how Christians worship."[17]

Some years ago, Craig Dykstra, presently vice president for religion at Lilly Endowment, Inc., and an ordained minister in the

Presbyterian Church (USA), began to focus attention on practices of faith that form us morally.[18] More recently, he has worked with Dorothy C. Bass, director of Valparaiso University's Project on the Education and Formation of People in Faith.[19] Dykstra and Bass define Christian practices as *"things people do together over time in response to and in the light of God's active presence for the life of the world."*[20] They assert, "Christian practices address needs that are basic to human existence."[21] This is precisely right. Those practices of our lives together in religious community, particularly in worship, are essential for positive human being and becoming.

In the following paragraphs, I am going to describe part of what is going on in the local parish where I worship. The practices of the Christian faith, the practices of empathy, that are present in a Roman Catholic Church are not precisely those of other Christian groups. In our formation as Friends, Baptists, Nazarenes, Unitarian Universalists or United Methodists, practices arise from the depths of tradition of each religious expression. So while I describe the practices of empathy within a Catholic Mass on Sunday at my local parish, I do not wish to say that the practices are identical or superior to those that you, the reader, bring to this book. I offer an analysis of my parish only because it is the one I know best.

Christian practices may be talked about in general, but the practices of Christian faith are specific to the religious traditions from which they arise. I imagine that my description arising from the context of my religious practice will give rise to reflection of those practices in your own religious setting. I will alert the reader to those Christian practices that I (we) enact each Sunday morning by highlighting each **practice**. This is an easy and fun exercise for you and your community of faith to try out. We know that the development of empathy is an essential guard against bullying— in individuals and in groups. To think of the life of the parish or congregation as preparing persons for doxological life is hopeful and exciting—that through the normal practices of Christian life in worship, we are learning how to be in relation with other persons in caring and hospitable ways. Once you pay attention to the practices of faith already present in your community, the question, "What is the purpose of these practices?" will invite insightful discussion about the ways empathy is nurtured.

Practicing Empathy at Worship

We are **greeted** at the door. We **walk with reverence** into the church, with its **carved** marble altar, **stained**-glass windows, and brilliantly **painted** ceiling. **Choosing a pew, we kneel on one knee** (genuflect) before entering the pew, and **sit down in an attitude of prayer and expectation. We stand** and face the center aisle as one of the leaders **extends greetings.** We **introduce** ourselves to those around us whom we do not know. Another worship leader invites us to a time of **confession** of sin, leading us in the **singing** of the Kyrie Eleison (Lord, have mercy…Christ, have mercy…Lord, have mercy). We in the congregation **respond by singing** the Kyrie—a **dialogue** between leadership and laity. Christ is present in the whole assembled body, not just the priest. Our **attention** is placed on no one ordained person, but on the gathered community as a whole. We **read** the words of a new hymn, and **sing along** with the choir. The pipe organ **plays.** We **smell** the incense **carried** by a layperson down the center aisle (placed below the lectern in front of the church), representing the prayers of the people "going up to God." We **remember** the liturgical colors of the year on stoles, on the lectern, on the altar. We **kneel to pray.** We **sit to hear** the Old Testament reading, and **respond** with the **singing** of Psalm 51. The epistle **reading** is followed by the **singing** of a song based on John 9. We **make a small sign** of the cross on our foreheads, our mouths, and our hearts as we **stand** (a symbol of resurrection) **to hear** the reading of the Gospel. We **listen** to the homily, an act of imagination and artistry. We **say from memory** the Nicene Creed. When I forget the words to the Nicene Creed, I **listen** to others, and I **remember. General intercessions** are made by a lay leader on behalf of the congregation. The morning **offering is collected.** Ushers **bring** the collected money to the front of the church. Lay members of the congregation **bring bread and wine** at the same time. A **prayer** is offered for the gifts. We **sing** "Amazing Grace." The **choir sings** an anthem, "Create in Me a Clean Heart." The priest consecrates the bread and wine. We **see** the bread and wine consecrated; **we remember.** We **hear** the words of the Last Supper. We see the **bread broken.**

We **prepare to pray** the Lord's Prayer by **holding hands** with the persons next to us. The man to my left reaches across the aisle to another man so that nobody will be left out. We **see** familiar friends. We **look** at the stained glass; **imagination soars.** We **pass the peace of Christ** with a **kiss,** with a **handshake,** with a **wave,** with a **smile,** with a **word of encouragement,** with a **hug,** whatever seems appropriate. I hear an eighteen-month-old child **cry out,** "Peace! Peace!" to everyone's delight. Gay and lesbian persons, homeless people with their ripped plastic bags of stuff, lawyers, teachers, old people, young people, babies, curious tourists who have never been in a church—all are **present**, all are **welcome**. During the passing of the peace, we **hear languages and accents** from around the world. There are many forms of **dress**: suits and ties, cutoff jeans, T-shirts and sandals, formal dresses and exquisite hats, Sylvester and Tweety halters and flip-flops. Emotionally troubled men **talk** to themselves in jerky motions; some talk with toothless mouths. **Thanks** is given to God.

We repent by saying together the Agnes Dei (Lamb of God…). Together we **say**, "Lord, I am not worthy to receive you, but only say the word, and I shall be healed." We **walk**, we **ride in wheelchairs**, and some of us are **carried to receive** the bread and wine. An African American woman in her late seventies with a neon-blue sequined beret **holds out** the bread (host) to me and **says**, "The Body of Christ." I **respond**, "Amen," as I **place** the bread (host) in my mouth, **cross** myself, and **return** to my pew—**changed**.

We **stand together**. We **look to the ceiling** painted with each of the twelve disciples, and **remember** gospel stories that the paintings **evoke**. **I especially like Andrew and his fish**. A baby **clunks** his head on the pew and **cries**—we **pray** for the mother, who may feel flustered, and for the baby, who is hurt and frightened. Opportunities for **social engagement** are **announced**, including political action, feeding the hungry, giving shelter to the homeless, religious education, choir rehearsal, and being Sunday morning ushers. Words of **welcome** to strangers are extended by the priest. We **clap** for strangers. We **stand** and **sing** "Hold Us in Your Mercy." The Eucharistic Minister comes up front to take the Eucharist to shut-in members on behalf of the congregation. **Announcements** about the work of the church are made. We are **blessed** in the name of the Father, the Son, and the Holy Spirit as we each **make the sign** of the cross. We are **dismissed** with the words, "The Mass has ended, now **go in peace**." **Worship** prepares us for a time of **mission**. The old woman in front of me takes out her red comb and **combs** her matted, thinning, pure-white hair. The homeless man next to me with a black eye and stringy hair **picks up** my bulletin and **asks**, "Did you **forget** this?" I had. We **chat**. He **tells** me that I am the first person with whom he has **talked** all week. His breath is heavy with stale cigarette smoke and alcohol.

We **share** punch and cookies downstairs. We **sign up to serve** the homeless persons who gather at the shelter in the church basement on Saturday nights, November through March. I **marvel** at God's abundant goodness. I **think** to myself, "This is an attempt, a very real attempt, to be distinctively Catholic. This is an attempt to practice caring for one another, for ourselves, for our relation with God, and for our relation to the world." I **leave** renewed. But I can hardly wait for the next time we worship together again in our diversity, one in Jesus Christ.

Reflections on Practices of Empathy at Worship

Worship is at the center of the Christian life, and public worship at my (our) parish on Sunday mornings is characterized by its distinct practices. I contend that these practices, when taken alone or together, provide education and training in empathy. It has been argued earlier in this book that empathy is at the heart of who God is for us in Jesus. Through our practices, we are responding to God's love in Jesus. Through our practices, we seek to be more like God in the world. Or said another way, we seek to embody those practices that are congruent with doxology, and by so doing, we become more empathetic. The general virtues of hospitality, friendship, and caring are composed of specific acts or practices. I am going to be guided in this discussion of general and specific practices by the research of the Valparaiso University Project.[22]

Hospitality

Welcoming Diversity. The church in which worship is described above is an urban parish. Its diversity is wonderfully doxological. The age range is from newborn babies to older adults in their late eighties. The languages spoken are from all over the world. The accents are full of dignity and speak of lands far away. Homeless people sit next to wealthy people. People with coats and ties or the fanciest of dresses sit next to people in halter-tops and flip-flops. Gay and lesbian people sit with straight people. Single parents are next to grandparents who are parenting their children's children. Black people from around the world are with Asian people from around the world. Middle Eastern folk sit with white Southerners whose families have been here for generations. I do not mean to suggest that all this diversity is always easy. But there we are together, one in Christ. Sometimes I watch all the people going forward for the Eucharist and I can hardly believe my eyes. We practice hospitality because it is Christian to accept one another in love. Our diversity is what we have most in common. Paradoxically, our diversity is our unity in Christ.

Economics. We collect money during the worship service as an act of hospitality. Reaching out to others unlike ourselves can be assisted by adequate funding. I have heard leaders in the ecumenical church respond cynically to the offering of gifts during a service of worship. They say that collecting money during worship is merely a celebration and affirmation of capitalism. While collecting the offering may degenerate into this, it need not be so. In a real sense, we are returning to God what is already God's. Taking a collection of money is more about stewardship than a celebration of an economic system. In fact, the collection of an offering is a critique of the accumulation of wealth for greed's sake.

At the parish, we know where the money that is collected is spent. The level of local, national, and international social services supported by the offering is significant. We know also that the time of offering is not only about money, but also about time and talents offered to the church's ministry during the week. We are reminded by one another and by the parish leadership that our "worth comes from God, not from money,"[23] and how our money may be used in the ongoing mission of the church—especially among the poor, the very young, and the very old.

At the same time, laity bring the gifts of bread and wine forward. We understand that we are all invited to this table to eat and that somehow the ordinary gift of food from God may become spiritual nourishment as well.

Discernment. When we are invited to reflect on the reasons we act as we do, we are opening our potential for hospitality. Closed-mindedness and closed communities go hand-in-hand. Particularly in the homily, we are asked to reflect on experience. Scripture, tradition, theology, and other perspectives are brought to bear on the challenges of Christian faith and life. Experience in itself is nothing much without interpretation. Theologian David Tracy has suggested, "to be human is to act reflectively, to decide deliberately, to understand intelligently, to experience fully. Whether we know it or not, to be human is to be a skilled interpreter."[24] In the Mass, we remember the life, death, and resurrection of Jesus. We remember the saints around us. We remember the new life of doxology. When we see liturgical colors, we remember the story of the Christian faith throughout the year, reminded of the whole story of Jesus Christ. This remembering is an active process of reflection on the opportunities for Christian living. We practice discernment in the church through the choices we make among ourselves for the ongoing mission of the church, as well as in our daily lives in mission. Religious education classes are offered on Sunday mornings in order to give persons the time and opportunity to hone their skills of Christian interpretation.

Memory is a very big part of Catholic worship. To the newcomer, worship may seem very complicated and confusing. The Nicene Creed, the Lord's Prayer, the "Lamb of God" prayer, or the "Lord, I am not worthy" prayer, how and when to make the sign of the cross, and when to stand or sit are repeated week after week. I never tire of saying the Nicene Creed. I learn something new about my belief every time I say it. Certainly, all of this memory can become stale. But as we recall our responsibility to interpret the faith and to consider the relation of faith and living, memory acts as an aid to deeper and deeper understanding. And when I forget parts of the creed, the community supports me!

Friendship

Forgiveness and Healing. Forgiveness is a major part of worship. We begin worship with a time of personal confession of sin. During the Eucharistic celebration (communion), we corporately and individually have opportunity for the confession of sin. During the Lord's Prayer, we remember to ask forgiveness of our trespasses as we forgive the trespasses of others. Every time we kneel, we are reminded of our need for humility and service. The act of holding hands during the Lord's Prayer and the act of passing the peace of Christ require special attention to one's relations with others. One's attitudes toward gay and lesbian persons, persons of different cultural identities, the homeless and the poor, and the rich and powerful take on a certain concreteness when holding hands or looking another person in the eyes.

Within the larger context of the life of the parish, the sacrament of penance and reconciliation is offered regularly. "Interior repentance" is an indication of desire and resolution to walk afresh in doxology.[25] With repentance comes forgiveness and healing.

Spiritual healing is always related to physical healing. There is no division in Catholic theology between mind, body, and spirit. The church's ministry to homeless men during the cold winter months and its ongoing ministry with various AIDS organizations in the city of Atlanta are public testimonies of the inter-connectedness of body and spirit. The parish is also part of a downtown effort to provide medical care for the poor and homeless, including the treatment of infected or damaged feet of homeless persons.

Caring

Honoring the Body. The human body is an instrument of worship. We walk, we kneel, we stand, we join hands, we kiss, we shake hands, we wave, we hug, we carry those who cannot walk, we welcome wheelchairs into the sanctuary, we clap, and we comb our hair. We have a shelter for homeless men (immediately beneath the sanctuary) during the cold months of year, where they may take a shower, eat a warm meal, sleep on a comfortable cot with mattress, and repair clothes. We eat during the worship service— the bread of the body of Christ,[26] as well as have punch and cookies after worship, providing a context for kinship and conversation. We make the sign of the cross with our arms and with our hands. We kneel, we look up, and we feel our voices sing. By accepting the fact that we have physical bodies, we remember our mortality as well as our joy of feeling. The woman who combed her hair with a red comb was taking pride in her appearance, in her physical self.

Dying Well. One of the things that has impressed me most about the kinship of persons at the parish is the dignity and respect offered to older adults. I have experienced an unexpected level of patience, acceptance, and caring for older adults. Included in this respect for the older adult is the visitation by a Eucharistic minister to the homes of shut-ins or ill folks. The Eucharistic minister is sent by the priest with the consecrated bread (host) to the person who cannot share in worship at the parish building.

Nurturing Awe, Wonder, and the Imagination

The Arts. Awe and wonder are signs of a healthy religious life. The child, young person, or adult whose outlook on life is grounded in awe and wonder has a way of seeing the world and others differently. Essential for the healthy development of empathy, the arts are primary ways for developing affective or emotional intelligence.[27] Sometimes, wonder can be a matter of ignorance, such as "I wonder why a homeless person would attend this Mass?" This is a completely appropriate kind of wonder. But there are other kinds of wonder too, such as, "I wonder how this church in its diversity is able to serve God with one heart?" This is a wonderment of marvel, one that asks the imagination to break out of old paradigms and old ways of thinking.[28] The arts invite us to be creative, to see in a new way.[29]

Our present church building was dedicated in 1873, and is attentive to the ways art teaches us. The sanctuary itself is in the shape of a cross. The ceiling has paintings of the twelve disciples, each outlined by a wooden trefoil (symbolizing the Trinity). The stained-glass windows along the sides of the sanctuary remind us of biblical stories and saints. The window above the altar is symbolic of Mary, mother of Jesus. Opposite this window is the choir loft, with pipe organ. The Stations of the Cross and old oil paintings line the walls of the sanctuary. A sculpture of Mary holding the dead Jesus stands near the front. In the back of the sanctuary is a beautiful baptismal font, flowing with water. One almost has to step into the font to enter the church!

On any Sunday morning, literature, music, the visual arts, and the arts of movement are somehow integrated into the Mass. The arts in this church building call all of us who worship there to a higher level of literacy (it is amazing how well one must know the Bible and church history in order to interpret the art), and a higher level of wonder. Could Mass go on without the arts? Of course, the Mass could go on. But the presence of the arts develops the capacity for the expression of feelings and emotions in a very special way.

A week ago, I enjoyed watching a young girl about eight years old who was seated in the front pew with her mother. There was so much to do, so much to see, so much to listen to from the choir, and so much to sing from the hymnbook that she craned her neck around and around in anticipation of what might happen next. As she departed the church, her mother had to direct her by the hand as the child could not take her eyes off the paintings on the ceiling!

The awe and wonder called forth by the arts encourage persons of all ages to feel and to think in new ways. The arts are essential in the church, public or private school, and home as a means for the education and training of the emotions. Violent video games that are artistic are not the same as the art of the church building, which invites an encounter with beauty and truths. The arts are essential in the healthy development of empathy.

Practicing Doxology

Hospitality (welcoming diversity, economics, discernment), friendship (forgiveness, healing), caring (honoring the body, dying well), and nurturing awe, wonder, and the imagination (the arts) are primary means of practicing empathy. If it is true that empathy is learned primarily through modeling by significant authority figures in our lives, I contend that the local church or parish is a significant public place in our culture for helping persons to learn to live together in empathetic ways. The practice of doxology is not easy, and sometimes local churches and parishes lose their ways. But a new awareness of the practices of Christian faith by the worshiping congregation could signal a renewal of understanding of the importance of faith communities in the repair of the violence and violation around the world. Inviting a congregation to examine its basic Christian practices is a practical way to "take stock" and to treasure its potential importance to the common good. The pattern of relationships we model in worship is a powerful teacher.

APPENDIX

Resources

Many academic resources have been offered in the endnotes of this book for further study and reflection. The resources in this appendix include more "hands-on" materials for use in the classroom, at home, in the religious education setting, or in a workshop. This bibliography is not intended to be exhaustive. I have included those resources I trust and that I find of particular value for those persons with whom I have worked on the topic of bullying. Remember that most of the resources I have listed here also have very good bibliographies.

Resources for Teachers

Besag, Valerie E. *Bullies and Victims in Schools: A Guide to Understanding and Management.* Milton Keynes, Eng., and Philadelphia: Open University Press, 1989.

Borba, Michele. *Esteem Builders: A K-8 Self-Esteem Curriculum for Improving Student Behavior and School Achievement.* Rolling Hills Estates, Calif.: Jalman Press, 1989.

Froschl, Merle, Barbara Sprung, Nancy Mullin-Rindler, with Nan Stein and Nancy Gropper. *Quit It! A Teacher's Guide on Teasing and Bullying for Use with Students in Grades K-3.* Washington, D. C.: National Education Association, 1998.

Garrity, Carla, et al. *Bully-Proofing Your School: A Comprehensive Approach for Elementary Schools.* Longmont, Colo.: Sopris West, 1995.

Goleman, Daniel. *Working with Emotional Intelligence.* New York: Bantam Books, 1998.

Hoover, John H., and Ronald Oliver. *The Bully Prevention Handbook: A Guide for Principals, Teachers, and Counselors.* Bloomington, Ind.: National Education Service, 1996.

Kreidler, William J. *Creative Conflict Resolution: More Than 200 Activities for Keeping Peace in the Classroom K-6.* Glenview, Ill.: Scott, Foresman and Company, 1984.

Meeks, Linda, et al. *Violence Prevention: Totally Awesome Teaching Strategies for Safe and Drug-Free Schools.* Blacklick, Ohio: Meeks Heit, 1995.

Olweus, Dan, and Susan P. Limber. *Blueprint for Violence Prevention: Book Nine. Bullying Prevention Program.* Denver, Colo.: C & M Press, 1999.

Palmer, Parker J. *The Courage to Teach: Exploring the Inner Landscape of a Teacher's Life.* San Francisco: Jossey-Bass, 1998.

Ross, Dorthea M. *Childhood Bullying and Teasing: What School Personnel, Other Professionals, and Parents Can Do.* Alexandria, Va.: American Counseling Association, 1996.

Stein, Nan, et al. *Bullyproof: A Teacher's Guide on Teasing and Bullying for Use with Fourth and Fifth Grade Students.* Washington, D. C.: National Education Association, 1996.

Resources for Children

Cheltenham Elementary School Kindergartners, *We Are All Alike…We Are All Different.* Photographs by Laura Dwight. New York: Scholastic Inc., 1991.

Cohen, Barbara. *Molly's Pilgrim.* Illustrated by Michael J. Deraney. New York: Bantam Doubleday Dell Books for Young Readers, 1983.

Coles, Robert. *The Story of Ruby Bridges.* Illustrated by George Ford. New York: Scholastic Inc., 1999.

hooks, bell, and Chris Raschka. *Happy to Be Nappy.* New York: Jump at the Sun/Hyperion Books for Children, 1999.

Johnson, Julie. *Bullies and Gangs.* Brookfield, Conn.: Copper Beech Books, 1998.

Lobe, Tamara Awad. *Let's Make a Garden.* Scottdale, Pa.: Herald Press, 1995.

McCain, Becky Ray. *Nobody Knew What to Do: A Story About Bullying.* Morton Grove, Ill.: Albert Whitman & Co., 2001.

Powell, Jillian. *Talking about Bullying.* Austin, Tex.: Raintree Steck-Vaughn, 1999.

Romain, Trevor. *Bullies Are a Pain in the Brain.* Edited by Elizabeth Verdick. Minneapolis: Free Spirit Publications, 1997.

Sherwood, Jonathan. *Painting the Fire.* Story by Liz Farrington, illustrated by Douglas Moran. Sausalito, Calif.: Enchanté, 1993.

www.bully.org ("Where You Are Not Alone").

Resources for Youth

Banfield, Susan. *Ethnic Conflicts in Schools.* Springfield, N. J.: Enslow, 1995.

Bridges, Ruby. *Through My Eyes.* New York: Scholastic, Inc., 1999.

Coombs, H. Samm. *Teenage Survival Manual.* Glen Ellen, Calif.: Halo Books, 2002.

Frank, Anne. *The Diary of a Young Girl: The Definitive Edition.* New York: Doubleday, 1995.

Kaufman, Gershen, et al. *Every Kid's Guide to Personal Power and Positive Self-Esteem.* Minneapolis: Free Spirit Publishing, 1999.

McGraw, Jay. *Life Strategies for Teens Workbook.* New York: Simon and Schuster, 2001.

Menhard, Roffé Francha. *School Violence: Deadly Lessons.* Berkeley Heights, N. J.: Enslow, 2000.

Merton, Thomas, ed. *Gandhi on Non-Violence: A Selection from the Writings of Mahatma Gandhi.* New York: New Directions, 1965.

Roberts, Anita. *Safe Teen: Powerful Alternatives to Violence.* Vancouver: Polestar Book Publishers, 2001.

Resources for Adults

Cappello, Dominic. *Ten Talks Parents Must Have with Their Children about Violence*. New York: Hyperion, 2000.

Condon, Camy, and James McGinnis. *Helping Kids Care: Harmony Building Activities for Home, Church, and School*. Bloomington, Ind.: The Institute for Peace and Justice and Meyer Stone Books, 1988.

Day, Nancy. *Violence in Schools: Learning in Fear*. Springfield, N. J.: Enslow, 1996.

Dillon, Ilene L. *Exploring Anger with Your Child*. Palo Alto, Calif.: Enchanté, 1994.

Hoertdoerfer, Patricia, and William Sinkford, eds. *Creating Safe Congregations: Toward an Ethic of Right Relations: A Workbook for Unitarian Universalists*. Boston: Unitarian Universalist Association, 1997.

McGinnis, Kathleen and James. *Parenting for Peace and Justice: Ten Years Later*. Maryknoll, N. Y.: Orbis Books, 1993.

Olweus, Dan. *Bullying at School: What We Know and What We Can Do*. Oxford: Blackwell, 1993.

Stern-LaRosa, Caryl, and Ellen Hofheimer Bettman. *Hate Hurts: How Children Learn and Unlearn Prejudice*. New York: Scholastic Inc., 2000.

Voors, William. *The Parent's Book About Bullying: Changing the Course of Your Child's Life, For Parents on Either Side of the Bullying Fence*. Center City, Minn.: Hazelden, 2000.

Wuellner, Flora Slosson. *Release: Healing from the Wounds of Family, Church, and Community*. Nashville: Upper Room Books, 1996.

Organizations to Contact for Further Information

The Anti-Defamation League
823 United Nations Plaza
New York, NY 10017
www.adl.org/

Center for the Study and Prevention of Violence
University of Colorado
http://www.colorado.edu/cspv/

Committee for Children
Information on Bullying and Sexual Harassment
www.cfchildren.org

Council for Spiritual and Ethical Education
1465 Northside Drive
Suite 220
Atlanta, Georgia 30318

Institute on Family and Neighborhood Life
Clemson University
158 Poole Agricultural Center
Clemson, North Carolina 29634–0132
(864)656–6271

The Lion and Lamb Peace Arts Center
Bluffton College
280 West College Avenue, Suite 1
Bluffton, Ohio 45817
(800) 488–3257

Maine Project Against Bullying
http://lincoln.midcoast.com/~wps/against/bullying.html
National Coalition Building Institute International
1835 K. Street N.W., Suite 715
Washington, D. C. 20006
(202) 785–9400

Parenting for Peace and Justice Network
The Institute for Peace and Justice
Families Against Violence Advocacy Network
www.ipj-ppj.org

Notes

Preface

[1]Tonja R. Nansel et al., "Bullying Behaviors Among U.S. Youth: Prevalence and Association with Psychosocial Adjustment," *The Journal of the American Medical Association* 285, no. 16, 2094–2100.

Chapter 1: Violence and Christian Life

[1]Peter Senge et al., *The Fifth Discipline Field Book: Strategies for Building a Learning Organization* (New York: Currency Doubleday, 1994), 3.

[2]Catherine Mowry LaCugna, *God For Us: The Trinity and Christian Life* (San Francisco: Harper San Francisco, 1991), 343.

[3]Ibid.

[4]Ibid.

[5]Mark Juergensmeyer, *Terror in the Mind of God: The Global Rise of Religious Violence* (Berkeley: University of California Press, 2000).

[6]Simone Weil, *The Iliad or the Poem of Force* (Wallingford, Pa.: Pendle Hill, 1983), 3.

[7] W. R. Johnson, *Momentary Monsters: Lucan and His Heroes* (Ithaca, N.Y.: Cornell University Press, 1987), 109. Johnson is referring here to the character of Caesar at the battle of Pharsalus during the Roman Civil War. See chapters 7 and 8 of Lucan, *Pharsalia*, trans. Jane Wilson Joyce (Ithaca, N.Y.: Cornell University Press, 1993), v. 647ff.

[8]The seminal work of Bronfenbrenner is not easily accessible. A simple summary of his approach to understanding human development may be found in Kelvin L. Seifert, Robert J. Hoffnung, and Michele Hoffnung, *Lifespan Development* (Boston: Houghton Mifflin Company, 2000), 8–9. A helpful visual model of this theory is provided on page 9. A more scholarly summary of his work may be found in Urie Bronfenbrenner and Stephen J. Ceci, "Nature–Nurture Reconceptualized in Developmental Perspective: A Bioecological Model," *Psychological Review* 101, no. 4 (1994): 568–86. The article includes a fine bibliography plus candid suggestions for future areas of inquiry.

[9]Jonathan Kozol, *Amazing Grace: The Lives of Children and the Conscience of a Nation* (New York: HaperPerennial, 1996).

[10]Jonathan Kozol, *Ordinary Resurrections: Children in the Years of Promise and Hope* (New York: Crown, 2000), 137ff.

[11]Kozol, *Amazing Grace*, 142.

[12]Kozol, *Ordinary Resurrections*, 155.

[13]The term *lockdown* comes from a provocative article written by theologian Mark Taylor, "The Executed God: The Way of the Cross in Lockdown America," *The Princeton Seminary Bulletin* 21, no. 3, new series (2000). Taylor first heard the term *lockdown* from a thirteen–year–old member of his church.

[14]Walter Brueggemann, *Theology of the Old Testament: Testimony, Dispute, Advocacy* (Minneapolis: Fortress Press, 1997), 747.

[15]Peter L. Berger and Thomas Luckmann, *The Social Construction of Reality: A Treatise in the Sociology of Knowledge* (New York: Doubleday and Company, 1967), 130.

[16]Parker Palmer, *To Know as We Are Known: A Spirituality of Education* (San Francisco: Harper and Row, 1983), 19.

[17]J. Christiaan Beker, *Paul the Apostle: The Triumph of God in Life and Thought* (Philadelphia: Fortress Press, 1980), 184.

[18]It can be argued that Matthew and Mark contain sacrificial motifs of the sort developed by Paul. It was Paul, however, who brought the scapegoat myth to flower theologically.

[19]J. Christiaan Beker explores the importance of Jewish assumption of "cursed be every one who hangs on a tree," for example. See Beker, *Paul the Apostle,* 202ff.

[20]J. Denny Weaver, *The Nonviolent Atonement* (Grand Rapids, Mich.: Eerdmans, 2001), 52. Weaver, an Anabaptist, concludes that "satisfaction atonement is based on divinely sanctioned, retributive violence" (225). In this, I am in agreement. But I am not convinced that Paul was equally convinced of this assertion, particularly in his later writings.

[21]B. Hudson McClean, *The Cursed Christ: Mediterranean Expulsion Rituals and Pauline Soteriology* (Sheffield, Eng.: Sheffield Academic Press, 1996), 105–7. John Dominic Crossan makes a similar claim of the importance of the scapegoat myth in regard to the synoptic gospels. See John Dominic Crossan, *The Cross That Spoke: The Origins of the Passion Narrative* (San Francisco: Harper & Row, 1988).

[22]By critical correlation, I refer to the theological method of David Tracy, *Blessed Rage for Order: The New Pluralism in Theology* (Chicago: University of Chicago Press, 1996).

[23]Paul was a critical and reflective theologian not interested in simply imitating culture. That Paul was a brilliant Christian theologian is not at issue here. What is at issue is the normativity of Pauline theology for the Christian church today. Near the heart of this matter is the issue of the formation of canon and what counts as canon, which is beyond the scope of this argument. As such, Paul's theology offers a case study to the Christian church of the relation of the meaning of the life and death of Jesus—and the ways this meaning is expressed to the culture in which we live.

[24]There has been significant biblical work applying the theory of René Girard to the interpretation of the Bible. It is my perspective that this approach to biblical interpretation simply reinforces a hermeneutic that was superimposed on the life and death of Jesus that leads to the misinterpretation of the gospel (especially at the point of atonement). This is a very different perspective from Girard himself. He writes in the forward of Gil Bailie, *Violence Unveiled: Humanity at the Crossroads* (New York: Crossroad, 1995), xii, "the close relativeness of gospel and myth is the means through which the uniqueness of the Judeo–Christian tradition is vindicated, not the means through which it is denied." For a sound and compelling approach to the use of Girard in the interpretation of the Bible, see James G. Williams, *The Bible, Violence, and the Sacred: Liberation from the Myth of Sanctioned Violence* (San Francisco: HarperSanFrancisco, 1991); and Robert G. Hamerton–Kelly, *The Gospel and the Sacred: Poetics of Violence in Mark* (Minneapolis: Fortress Press, 1994).

[25]The most "user–friendly" introduction to Girard that I have found is by Richard J. Golsan, *An Introduction to René Girard and Myth* (New York: Routledge, 2002).

[26]This notion of mimesis is congruent with the definition of sin offered by the *Catechism of the Catholic Church* (New York: Image, 1995), 505, "failure in genuine love for God and neighbor caused by a perverse attachment to certain goods." Mimesis as a general category of literary analysis (imitation) is ancient. See John D. Lyons and Stephen G. Nichols, Jr., eds., *Mimesis: From Mirror to Method, Augustine to Descartes* (Hanover, N.H.: University Press of New England, 1982).

[27]Toril Moi, "The Missing Mother: The Oedipal Rivalries of René Girard," *Diacritics* 12 (1982): 22. While beyond the scope of this chapter, Moi convincingly wonders about the adequacy of Girard to take into account the experience of women. See 21–31.

[28]René Girard, *Des Choses Cachées Depuis la Fondation du Monde* (Paris: B. Grasset, 1978), 393.

[29]René Girard, *Violence and the Sacred* (Baltimore: The Johns Hopkins University Press, 1977), 259.

[30]René Girard, *The Scapegoat* (Baltimore: The Johns Hopkins University Press, 1989), 17–20ff, 198.

[31]Ibid., 42.

[32]Markus Mueller, "Interview With René Girard," *Anthropoetics* 2, no. 1 (June 1996): 6. Accessed February 13, 2002, http://www.anthropoetics.ucla.edu/AP0201/home.html

[33]Girard, *The Scapegoat*, 205–6.

[34]Ibid., 206.

[35]This is a reformulation of the Reformation statement by Martin Luther, "Knowledge of God comes into being at the cross of Christ," as quoted in Walther von Loewenich, *Luther's Theology of the Cross* (Minneapolis: Augsburg, 1976), 20.

[36]René Girard, *I See Satan Fall Like Lightning* (Maryknoll, N.Y.: Orbis Books, 2001), 135.

[37]W. R. Johnson, *Momentary Monsters: Lucan and His Heroes*, 126–27.

[38]Desmond Tutu, "Justice, Memory and Reconciliation," 4, http://www.newsandevents.utoronto.ca/bin/000216a.asp, accessed February 1, 2002.

[39]One could ask the question, based on the many images of a God of violence in the Old Testament, whether this approach to understanding God (let alone to being created in God's image) is theologically or biblically adequate. By implicitly rejecting the notion of violence as inherent in the nature of God, am I presenting a sanitized version of who God is? This is a crucial hermeneutical issue. I contend that while human projections of violence onto God are very much in evidence in the Old Testament, they must be acknowledged as such—human projections. A God of fickle violence, whose abuse is randomly interspersed with "I love you, but sometimes I may abuse you for your own good or by whim" requires always a scapegoat to assuage [his] anger. Such a God calls forth destructive dependence, nothing more. In the words of Albert Memmi in *Dependence: A Sketch for a Portrait of the Dependent* (Boston: Beacon Press, 1984), 64, "In truth, there is something tragic about dependence. When one person is dependent on another, both the dependent and the provider live in the shadow of death. The dependent believes, rightly or wrongly, that negligence on the part of the provider would bring about her, the dependent's destruction; and rather than perish she would kill the provider." For an alternative view, see David R. Blumenthal, *Facing the Abusing God: A Theology of Protest* (Louisville: Westminster/John Knox Press, 1993).

[40]Beyond the limits of this book, Sarah Kofman gives rigorous critique of Girard's interpretation of Freud at just this point in her article, "The Narcissistic Woman: Freud and Girard," *Diacritics* 10 (1980): 42.

[41]Sarah Kofman notes the deficiency of the triadic understanding of mimesis from a feminist perspective. In an analysis of Girard's interpretation of Freud (with the resulting conclusion that women cannot be self-sufficient, and that female self-sufficiency is deceitful), Kofman reveals that sexism is at the core of Girard's understanding of mimesis. She writes, "But to be sure, woman as penis envier would not be able to inspire man's mimetic rivalry," in *The Enigma of Woman: Woman in Freud's Writings* (Ithaca, N.Y.: Cornell University Press, 1985), 65.

[42]I have not addressed the theology of Reinhold Niebuhr in this chapter. Sin being placed within the context of pride has been evaluated by Carol Lakey Hess, *Caretakers of Our Common House: Women's Development in Communities of Faith* (Nashville: Abingdon Press, 1997), 35, "When sin as pride is generalized, self-abnegation is rendered a virtue and harmfully reinforced." The absurdity of the notion of self-abnegation as sin would only detract from this chapter's focus. However, the matter will be addressed forthrightly in chapter 3.

[43]B. Hudson McLean, *The Cursed Christ*, 206–7.

[44]Marjorie Suchocki, *The Fall to Violence: Original Sin in Relational Theology* (New York: Continuum, 1994), 144.

[45]Theologian Richard McBrien summarizes this matter cogently in *Catholicism* (San Francisco: HarperSanFrancisco, 1994), 446. He writes, "Jesus was [not] marked out for death by the Father in expiation for offenses against the divine majesty, for neither is there any Old Testament model for such a notion." At the same time, from my perspective, McBrien offers inadequate justification of the cross in Pauline theological discourse.

[46]Rita Nakashima Brock and Rebecca Ann Parker, *Proverbs of Ashes: Violence, Redemptive Suffering, and the Search for What Saves Us* (Boston: Beacon Press, 2001), 157.

[47]Delores S. Williams, *Sisters in the Wilderness: The Challege of Womanist God–talk* (Maryknoll, N.Y.: Orbis Books, 1993), 167.

[48]Brock and Parker, *Proverbs of Ashes*, 157.

[49]Elie Wiesel, *Night* (New York: Bantam Books, 1982), 61–62.

[50]Seward Hiltner, "Moral Development as Paradox," unpublished address delivered at the Menninger Foundation on "Moral Development and Its Failures," Topeka, Kansas, October 18–19, 1979, 1.

[51]The sense of awe and peace in the presence of no–thing–ness is not far removed from the notion of the numinous in the works of Rudolf Otto. See Rudolf Otto, *The Idea of the Holy: An Inquiry into the Non–Rational Factor in the Idea of the Divine and Its Relation to the Rational* (New York: Oxford University Press, 1928). Otto writes, "For 'Void' is, like Darkness and Silence, a negation, but a negation that does away with every 'this' and 'here', in order that the 'wholly other' may become actual" (72).

[52]Lutheran theologian Eberhard Juengel comes to a very similar conclusion regarding my understanding of paradox in his book *God as the Mystery of the World: On the Foundation of the Theology of the Crucified One in the Dispute between Theism and Atheism* (Edinburgh, Scot.: T.&T. Clark, Ltd., 1983), 104. He writes, "But God's presence can only be experienced simultaneously with his absence."

[53]Dorothee Soelle, *Death by Bread Alone: Texts and Reflections on Religious Experience*, trans. David L. Scheit (Philadelphia: Fortress Press, 1978), 66.

[54]Sharon G. Thornton, *Broken Yet Beloved: A Pastoral Theology of the Cross* (St. Louis: Chalice Press, 2002), 129.

[55]Jose Miguez Bonino, *Christians and Marxists: The Mutual Challenge to Revolution* (Grand Rapids, Mich.: Eerdmans, 1976), 40–41.

[56]Christine Gudorf, *Victimization: Examining Christian Complicity* (Philadelphia: Trinity Press International, 1992), 28.

[57]In the early church it was thought that martyrs went to heaven immediately, rather than having to wait for the second coming of Jesus. While this particular background for the glorification of martyrdom has evaporated in contemporary times in most places, the residue of social prestige within the religious community remains widespread. See Sandra Sizer Frankiel, "Christianity: A Way of Salvation," in *Religions of the World*, ed. H. Byron Earhart (San Francisco: HarperSanFrancisco, 1992), 502.

[58]Shannon P. Daley and Kathleen A. Guy, *Welcome the Child: A Child Advocacy Guide for Churches* (New York: Friendship Press and Children's Defense Fund, 1994), 38.

[59]See Edna Maluma, "Abundant Life for Women and Children?" in *Claiming the Promise: African Churches Speak*, ed. Margaret S. Larom (New York: Friendship Press, 1994), 57–70.

[60]Wiesel, *Night*, 62.

[61]Kathleen M. O'Connor, *Lamentations and the Tears of the World* (Maryknoll, N.Y.: Orbis, 2002), 94.

[62]One may conclude from O'Connor that God's absence is just that—God's absence. It is my perspective that this kind of bipolar thinking (either God is present or God is absent) limits our understanding of the work of God unnecessarily. Paradox seeks no such simple dichotomy.

[63]Brock and Parker, *Proverbs of Ashes*, 156.

[64]Cheryl A. Kirk–Duggan, referring to the work of Christine Gudorf, makes a very similar assertion in *Refiner's Fire: A Religious Engagement with Violence* (Minneapolis: Fortress Press, 2001), 33–34. See also Christine E. Gudorf, *Victimization*.

[65]Susan Ford Wiltshire, *Public and Private in Vergil's Aeneid* (Amherst: The University of Massachusetts Press, 1989), 83.

[66]M. M. Bakhtin, *The Dialogic Imagination: Four Essays*, ed. Michael Holquist, trans. Caryl Emerson and Michael Holquist (Austin: University of Texas Press, 1981), 66–67.

[67]LaCugna, *God for Us*, 344.

[68]Toni Morrison, *Playing in the Dark: Whiteness and the Literary Imagination* (New York: Vintage Books, 1993). See also Philip L. Wickeri, "Friends Along the Way: Spirituality, Human Relationships and Christian Mission," *Theology* (May–June, 1990): 181–90.

[69]Morrison, *Playing in the Dark*, 73ff.

[70]Elie Wiesel, *Night*, 113

[71]Robert Coles, "The Moral Life of Children," *Agnes Scott Alumnae Magazine* (Fall 1989): 16.

[72]As quoted in *Catechism of the Catholic Church*, 365.

[73]More accurately stated, texts written by Paul, and texts attributed to Paul.

Chapter 2: Karl's Fall to Violence

[1]There is much contemporary legal debate about "onlookers" who fail to report crimes. Paraphrasing defense attorney Steve Sadow, newspaper reporter Beth Warren writes, "It may be immoral, but it's not criminal to watch a crime," Beth Warren, "Teen Charged as a Party to Sexual Assault," *Atlanta Journal-Constitution*, May 24, 2002, C4.

[2]A recent summary of research in this regard may be found in M. L. Cooper, R. Shaver, and N. L. Collins, "Attachment Styles, Emotion Regulation, and Adjustment in Adolescence," *Journal of Personality and Social Psychology* 74 (1998): 1380–97.

[3]Many good resources on adolescence are available. One of the most helpful to me is Tom Beaudoin, *Virtual Faith: The Irreverent Spiritual Quest of Generation X* (San Francisco: Jossey–Bass Publishers, 1998).

[4]Ann Swidler, "Culture in Action: Symbols and Strategies," *American Sociological Review* 51 (1986): 273.

[5]I do not wish to imply that private schools are always violence–free and that public schools are always filled with violence! This is not the case. I am aware of many religious private schools confronted with the problem of bullying, and I know of many public schools where attention to human relations is exemplary. The issue is culture–switching and its profound effects on young people.

[6]In the (Roman) Catholic Church, confirmation follows baptism. For children, baptism is a prerequisite of confirmation. For most children today, confirmation takes place in the eighth grade (age 13–14). At the time of Karl's confirmation, children would have been confirmed between sixth and eighth grades (age 11–14). In subsequent conversation with Karl, I learned that he had been confirmed before attending public school. For adults who choose to become Catholic, baptism is followed by confirmation, which is followed immediately by the Eucharist.

[7]While I have never seen the movements of ritual outlined in this precise way, it is a part of my Catholic "inner sense of being." A more scholarly approach may be found in Roy A. Rappaport, *Ritual and Religion in the Making of Humanity* (Cambridge, U.K.: Cambridge University Press, 1999). The discerning reader of Rappaport will notice the simple movements I have outlined in this chapter.

[8]Elie Wiesel, "Learning and Respect: A Challenge to Graduates," http://www.humanity.org/voices/commencements/speeches/index.php?page=wiesel_at_depaul, accessed September 11, 2001.

[9] Maxim Gorky, *Creatures That Once Were Men* (New York: Boni and Liveright, 1918).

[10] Ronald H. Cram, "Knowing God: Children, Play, and Paradox," *Religious Education* 91, no. 1 (1996): 63–67.

[11] See, for example, Alice Miller, *The Drama of the Gifted Child: The Search for the True Self* (New York: Basic Books, 1994); Judith Rich Harris, *The Nurture Assumption: Why Children Turn Out the Way They Do—Parents Matter Less Than You Think and Peers Matter More* (New York: The Free Press, 1998); Karen Horney, *New Ways in Psychoanalysis* (New York: W.W. Norton, 1939); and D. W. Winnicott, *Playing and Reality* (New York: Tavistock/Routledge, 1991).

[12] In the categories of Bronfenbrenner that we have been using, it was a person in the exosystem who intervened when all face-to-face support systems failed.

Chapter 3: Bullying as Spiritual Crisis

[1] Tonja R. Nansel et al., "Bullying Behaviors Among U.S. Youth: Prevalence and Association with Psychosocial Adjustment," *The Journal of the American Medical Association* 285, no. 16 (2001): 2094. There is an exhaustive reference listing that may be used by those persons interested in research from around the world.

[2] Ronald Hecker Cram, "Memories by Christian Adults of Childhood Bullying Experiences: Implications for Adult Religious Self–Understanding," *Religious Education* 96, no. 3 (2001): 326–49. This is the summary of a qualitative project. Empirical work within the context of the local parish or church remains untouched.

[3] I have offered workshops on the topic of bullying all over the country, and this observation tends to hold true. In addition, far more women than men turn out for discussion about violence, far more racial/ethnic persons than Anglo persons attend, and far more persons of religious traditions other than Christianity attend than Christians.

[4] A recent significant attempt to help raise consciousness about appropriate patterns of behavior in the life of the church is Flora Slosson Wuellner, *Release: Healing from Wounds of Family, Church and Community* (Nashville: Upper Room Books, 1996).

[5] Becky Ray McCain, *Nobody Knew What to Do: A Story about Bullying*, illust. Todd Leonardo (Morton Grove, Ill.: Albert Whitman, 2001).

[6] Nansel, "Bullying Behaviors Among U.S. Youth," 2094–2100.

[7] Darcia Harris Bowman, "Report Says Schools Often Ignore Harassment of Gay Students," *Education Week* 20, no. 39: 5.

[8] Herbert W. Marsh, Roberto H. Parada, Alexander Seeshing Yeung, and Jean Healy, "Aggressive School Troublemakers and Victims: A Longitudinal Model Examining the Pivotal Role of Self–Concept," *Journal of Educational Psychology* 93, no. 2: 411.

[9] Ibid.

[10] For a solid review of the relation of peers and bullying, see Ken Rigby, *New Perspectives on Bullying* (London: Jessica Kingsley, 2002), 163–68.

[11] Lyndal Bond, John B. Carlin, Lyndal Thomas, Kerryn Rubin, George Patton, "Does Bullying Cause Emotional Problems? A Prospective Study of Young Teenagers," *British Medical Journal* 233, no. 7311: 480–84.

[12] Karen S. Peterson, "When School Hurts: Continued Violence Has Schools, States Taking a Hard Look at Bullying," *USA Today*, 10 April 2001, sec. D.

[13] One person I interviewed took the initiative, on the basis of our conversation about bullies, to take a plane to another state, to track down the person by whom she had been bullied as a child, and to confront him. The childhood bully remembered the person whom he had bullied, but could not recall that any inappropriate behavior had taken place.

[14]Howard Spivak and Deborah Prothrow-Stith, "The Need to Address Bullying—An Important Component of Violence Prevention," *The Journal of the American Medical Association* 285, no. 16: 2131–32.

[15]An excellent study in this regard, with extensive bibliography, is Carolyn E. Roecker Phelps, "Children's Responses to Overt and Relational Aggression," *Journal of Clinical Child Psychology* 30, no. 1: 240–522.

[16]Ibid., 247–48.

[17]Martin J. Dunn, "Break the Bullying Cycle," *American School & University* 73, no. 10: 38–39.

[18]I can find little data to support this assertion, though I have heard it again and again from adults whom I have interviewed. Some bystanders are attracted to violence and enjoy seeing others hurt. But the feelings of those persons who feel compassion for others are significantly similar to those who are bullied. One compelling source that begins to address this issue is Ken Rigby, *Bullying in Schools: And What to Do About It* (London, Pa.: Jessica Kingsley, 1996), 65.

[19]Joan Wallach Scott, "The New University: Beyond Political Correctness," *Perspectives* 30, no. 7 (October 1992): 18.

[20]Stephen Kautz, "Liberalism and the Idea of Toleration," *American Journal of Political Science* 37, no. 2 (May 1993): 610.

[21]Ibid.

[22]Richard Rorty, *Consequences of Pragmatism* (Minneapolis: University of Minnesota Press, 1982), 203.

[23]Herbert Marcuse, "Repressive Tolerance," in Robert Paul Wolff, Barrington Moore, Jr., and Herbert Marcuse, *A Critique of Pure Tolerance* (Boston: Beacon Press, 1969), 81, 88.

[24]Bruce W. Speck, "Relativism and the Promise of Tolerance," *Journal of Interdisciplinary Studies* 10, nos. 1–2 (1998): 67. See also Arthur M. Melzer, "Tolerance 101," *The New Republic* (July 1, 1991): 11.

[25]David Hollenbach, S. J., "Is Tolerance Enough? The Catholic University and the Common Good," *Conversations on Jesuit Higher Education*, no. 13, spring 1998: 8.

[26]Eleanor R. Hall, Judith A. Howard, and Sherrie L. Boezio, "Tolerance of Rape: A Sexist or Antisocial Attitude?" *Psychology of Women Quarterly* 10, 1986: 101–2.

[27]Henry F. May, *The Enlightenment in America* (New York: Oxford University Press, 1976), 337.

[28]John Rawls, "The Idea of Overlapping Consensus," *Oxford Journal of Legal Studies* 7, no.1 (1987): 1, 2.

[29]Ibid., 3.

[30]Ibid., 7.

[31]Ibid., 4–5, 17.

[32]Ibid., 17.

[33]Susan Mendus, *Toleration and the Limits of Liberalism* (London: Macmillan, 1989), 114–17.

[34]Ibid., 108.

[35]This distinction was made by Michael Kinnamon, Allen and Dottie Miller Professor of Mission and Peace at Eden Theological Seminary, at a lecture on ecumenics at Columbia Theological Seminary, Georgia, in March 1999. While not addressing the topic of this chapter, the simple distinction is valuable.

[36]Theologian Anne E. Carr suggests that the Enlightenment brought with it an "anthropology of autonomy and self-creation." See *Transforming Grace: Christian Tradition and Women's Experience* (New York: Continuum, 1996), 158.

[37]Lucinda A. Stark Huffaker, *Creative Dwelling: Empathy and Clarity in God and Self* (Atlanta: Scholars Press, 1998), 71.

[38]Milton J. Bennett, "Overcoming the Golden Rule: Sympathy and Empathy," in his *Basic Concepts of Intercultural Communication: Selected Readings*, (Yarmouth, Maine: Intercultural Press, 1998), 191–213.

[39]Stanley Fish, "Condemnation Without Absolutes," *The New York Times on the Web*, October 15, 2001, 1–3, http://www.nytimes.com/2001/10/15/opinion/15FISH.html?pagewanted=print. Accessed October 15, 2001, requires registration to access.

[40]Edward Farley, *Divine Empathy: A Theology of God* (Minneapolis: Fortress Press, 1996), 282.

[41]Ibid., 281.

[42]Jon L. Berquist, *Incarnation* (St. Louis: Chalice Press, 1999), 29.

[43]Jeffrey Kluger, "Preventive Parenting: Paying Attention to a Baby's Unique Personality May Head Off Problems Before They Happen," *Time* (January 21, 2002): 87.

[44]Oscar Romero, "The Political Dimension of Christian Love," *Commonweal* (March 26, 1982): 171.

[45]Carol Lakey Hess, *Caretakers of Our Common House: Women's Development in Communities of Faith* (Nashville: Abingdon Press, 1997), 48.

[46]William Butler Yeats, "The Second Coming," in *The Collected Poems of W. B. Yeats* (New York: Macmillan, 1956), 184.

[47]Matthew 15:26, note h, *New Jerusalem Bible*, (New York: Doubleday, 1990), 1635.

[48]In Mary Ann Tolbert's analysis of "Mark" attention is given to the parallel story of the Syrophoenician woman in Mark 7:24–30. Tolbert concludes that the use of "dog" may be related to the philosophical movement of the Cynics. While the argument has merit, and while Tolbert concludes that Jesus learned from the woman, it is unlikely that Jesus' negative reaction to the woman in the beginning of the story is merely "role play." It is my view that such an interpretation misses the violence and force of the racism and sexism of Jesus. See Mary Ann Tolbert, "Mark," *The Women's Bible Commentary*, ed. Carol A. Newsom and Sharon Ringe (London: SPCK, 1992), 269.

[49]Sam Keen, *Faces of the Enemy: Reflections of the Hostile Imagination* (San Francisco: Harper and Row, 1986), 25.

[50]For some readers, this analysis of this biblical passage will be difficult because Jesus very often is portrayed as without sin or perfect. Jesus was fully human. Part of what it means to be human is to sin—and to engage in the process of conversion. Our brother Jesus shows us the meaning of salvation by sharing with us the gift of his life, including doxology and sin.

[51]Marie McCarthy, "Empathy Amid Diversity: Problems and Possibilities," *Journal of Pastoral Theology* 3 (1993): 21. It must be noted that empathy is not merely projection nor transference, though it is related to both. Michael J. Tansey and Walter F. Burke write in *Understanding Countertransference: From Projective Identification to Empathy* (Hillsdale, N.J.: The Analytic Press, 1989), 195: "Empathy is the outcome of a radically mutual interactive process between patient and therapist in which the therapist receives and processes projective identifications from the patient." Empathy includes a growing ability to reflect on one's perceptions. See Kenneth Bullmer, *The Art of Empathy: A Manual for Improving Accuracy of Interpersonal Perception* (New York: Human Sciences Press, 1975).

[52]H. Edward Everding and Lucinda A. Huffaker, "Educating Adults for Empathy: Implications of Cognitive Role–Taking and Identity Formation," *Religious Education* 93, no. 4 (fall 1998): 421. It may be that the current interest in mentoring is related directly to "teaching" empathy. See Susan B. Thistlethwaite and George F. Cains, eds., *Beyond Theological Tourism: Mentoring as a Grassroots Approach to Theological Education* (Maryknoll, N.Y.: Orbis Books, 1994).

[53]Nel Noddings, "The Cared For," in *Caregiving: Readings in Knowledge, Practice, Ethics, and Politics* (Philadelphia: University of Pennsylvania Press, 1996), 22.

[54]Nel Noddings, *The Challenge to Care in Schools: An Alternative Approach to Education* (New York: Teachers College Press, 1992), xi.

[55]Nel Noddings, "The Cared For," 27.

[56]Nel Noddings, *Philosophy of Education* (Boulder, Colo.: Westview Press, 1995), 188.

[57]Eleanor Humes Haney, "What Is Feminist Ethics: A Proposal for Continuing Discussion," *Journal of Religious Ethics* (spring 1980): 118.

[58]Mary E. Hunt, "Lovingly Lesbian: Toward a Feminist Theology of Friendship," *A Challenge to Love: Gay and Lesbian Catholics in the Church*, ed. Robert Nugent (New York: Crossroad, 1983), 135–55.

[59]Janice G. Raymond, *A Passion for Friends: Toward a Philosophy of Female Affection* (Boston: Beacon Press, 1986), 218.

[60]Roberta C. Bondi, "Friendship with God," *Weavings* (May–June 1992): 12.

[61]C. G. Jung, *Modern Man in Search of a Soul*, trans. W. S. Dell and C. F. Baynes (New York: Harcourt, Brace & Co., 1933), 235.

[62]Religion News Service, "Buddhists to Pray for Taliban," *The Atlanta Journal–Constitution*, 21 April 2001, B5.

[63]Ibid.

[64]David W. Augsburger, *Helping People Forgive* (Louisville: Westminster John Knox Press, 1996), 7.

[65]Jon Sobrino, "Latin America: Place of Sin and Place of Forgiveness," in *Forgiveness*, ed. Casiano Floristán and Christian Duquoc (Edinburgh, Scotland: T&T Clark, 1986), 45.

[66]As quoted in "On Winnie Madikizela–Mandela," accessed on http://news.bbc.co.uk on March 6, 2002.

[67]As quoted in Desmond Tutu, *No Future Without Forgiveness* (New York: Doubleday, 1999), 137.

[68]John Patton, *Is Human Forgiveness Possible? A Pastoral Care Perspective* (Nashville: Abingdon Press, 1985), 148.

[69]Beverly Flanigan, "Forgivers and the Unforgivable," in *Exploring Forgiveness*, ed. Robert D. Enright (Madison, Wis.: University of Wisconsin Press, 1998), 100.

[70]Thomas H. Groome, *Christian Religious Education: Sharing Our Story and Vision* (San Francisco: Harper and Row, 1980), 12.

[71]Marjorie Suchocki, *The Fall to Violence: Original Sin in Relational Theology* (New York: Continuum, 1994), 153.

[72]Peter Gilmour, *The Wisdom of Memoir: Reading and Writing Life's Sacred Texts* (Winona, Minn.: St. Mary's Press, 1997), 80.

[73]John Paul II, *Tertio Millennio Adveniente*, paragraph 35. Apostolic letter found at http://www.vaticano.va, accessed October 21, 2001.

[74]International Theological Commission, *Memory and Reconciliation: The Church and the Faults of the Past*, at http://www.vaticano.va/roman_curia/congregations/cfaith/cti_ documents/rc_con_cfaith_doc_20000307_memory–reconc–itc_en.html, 4 of 34. Accessed March 7, 2002.

[75]The Vatican's preparation for the Jubilee year of 2000 was truly remarkable in regard to interreligious concerns. The March 1998 document from the Commission for Religious Relations with the Jews, *We Remember: A Reflection on the Shoah*, presented by the president of the commission, Cardinal Edward Idris Cassidy, was another example of work completed in response to *Tertio Millennio Adveniente*. See http://www.vaticano.va/roman_curia/pontifical_councils/chrstuni/documents/rc_pc_chrstuni_doc_16031998_shoah_en.html

[76]http://www.vaticano.va/roman_curia/congregations/cfaith/documents/rc_con_cfaith_doc_20000806_dominus–iesus_en.html Accessed March 7, 2002.

[77]Some would find this evaluation flippant and inaccurate. It is, however, the only evaluation I can make regarding this very unfortunate ecclesial outburst.

[78]As this book goes to press, information related to child abuse within the priesthood in the United States continues to surface. Patterns of behavior within the male hierarchical system of the Roman Catholic church reflect denial, institutional maintenance over human dignity, disregard for the safety of children, hiding, and blaming those who have been victimized. Those who abused children,

as well as the church hierarchy are enacting patterns of bullying. The church seems both unable and unwilling to confess its sin, repent, and move into new patterns of life. Should this pattern of bullying continue, and should the violence of bullying become increasingly institutionalized, the church will affirm the ways of sin over the ways of doxology. How different this scenario might become if the pattern of repentance and forgiveness exemplified in the South African Truth and Reconciliation process were engaged.

[79]L. Gregory Jones, *Embodying Forgiveness: A Theological Analysis* (Grand Rapids, Mich.: William B. Eerdmans, 1995), 175.

[80]John Patton, *Is Human Forgiveness Possible?*, 147 ff.

[81]James E. Loder, *The Transforming Moment: Understanding Convictional Experiences* (San Francisco: Harper and Row, 1984), 54.

[82]Andrew Sung Park, *The Wounded Heart of God: The Asian Concept of Han and the Christian Doctrine of Sin* (Nashville: Abingdon Press, 1993), 170.

[83]Robert Kegan, *The Evolving Self: Problem and Process in Human Development* (Cambridge, Mass.: Harvard University Press, 1982), 89.

Chapter 4: Ways of Practicing Empathy

[1]Ken Rigby, *Bullying in Schools: And What to Do about It*, (Condon, Pa.: Jessica Kingsley, 1996) 80.

[2]Ibid., 136–38.

[3]Tom Lickona, Eric Schaps, and Catherine Lewis, "Eleven Principles of Effective Character Education," http://www.character.org/principles/index.cgi Accessed March 19, 2002. The Character Education Partnership is a major research and educational organization for schools.

[4]For a summary of present philosophical understandings of the relation between universals and fixed standards, see William B. Stanley, *Curriculum for Utopia: Social Reconstructionism and Critical Pedagogy in the Postmodern Era* (Albany, N.Y.: SUNY Press, 1992), 210.

[5]Saint Gregory of Nyssa, *The Lord's Prayer and The Beatitudes*, trans. Hilda C. Graef (Westminster, Md.: The Newman Press, 1954), 89.

[6]Ibid., 125.

[7]*Catechism of the Catholic Church* (New York, Image, 1995), 495–97.

[8]Ibid., 497–503.

[9]For this perspective I am indebted to J. L. Leming, "On the Limits of Rational Moral Education," *Theory and Research in Social Education* 9, no. 1 (1981): 7–34. Leming questions equating moral education with decision making alone. A just communal life, he argues, is essential for moral education to bear fruit.

[10]Brian S. Hook and R. R. Reno, *Heroism and the Christian Life: Reclaiming Excellence* (Louisville: Westminster John Knox Press, 2000), 203–20.

[11]E. B. White, *The Trumpet of the Swan* (New York: Harper & Row, 1970).

[12]The discerning reader will see many similarities between White's character Louis, a swan with no voice who plays a stolen trumpet, and Lawrence Kohlberg's classic "Heinz dilemma." See Lawrence Kohlberg, *The Psychology of Moral Development: The Nature and Validity of Moral Stages*, 1 (San Francisco: Harper & Row, 1984), 12–28. A religious understanding of cognitive moral reasoning is offered in Edward Everding et al., *Viewpoints: Perspectives of Faith and Christian Nurture* (Harrisburg, Pa.: Trinity Press International, 1998). It is important to note that cognitive moral development is not necessarily related to chronological time. That is, many adults may reason morally in ways similar to seven-year-old children.

[13]Catholic educational theorist Florence B. Stratemeyer developed this idea of persistent life situations for use in public schools. I believe the idea is equally important for religious educational settings. See Florence B. Stratemeyer et al., *Developing a Curriculum for Modern Living*, 2d ed. (New York: Bureau of Publications, Teachers College, Columbia University, 1957).

[14]Ethicist Marcia Y. Riggs elucidates the relation of teleological, deontological, responsibility, and liberation paradigms to ethical understanding in "Living Into Tensions: Christian Ethics as Mediating Process," in *Many Voices, One God: Being Faithful in a Pluralistice World*, ed. Walter Brueggemann and George Stroup (Louisville: Westminster John Knox Press, 1998), 181–92.

[15]Catherine Mowry LaCugna, *God for Us: The Trinity and Christian Life* (San Francisco: Harper SanFrancisco, 1991), 343.

[16]Paramount Pictures, 2002. The U.S. Army announced in 2002 that it would begin production soon of downloadable video games "Soldiers" and "Operations." The Army's announcement coincided with a television news story about increasing use by the U.S. military of video games for training of troops.

[17]Don E. Saliers, "Liturgy and Ethics: Some New Beginnings," in *Liturgy and the Moral Self: Humanity at Full Stretch Before God: Essays in Honor of Don E. Saliers*, ed. E. Byron Anderson and Bruce T. Morrill (Collegeville, Minn.: Liturgical Press, 1998), 15.

[18]Craig R. Dykstra, *Vision and Character: A Christian Educator's Alternative to Kohlberg* (New York: Paulist Press, 1981). His more recent contribution is *Growing in the Life of Christian Faith: Education and Christian Practices* (Louisville: Geneva Press, 1999).

[19]http://www.practicingourfaith.com, accessed March 12, 2002.

[20]Dorothy C. Bass, ed., *Practicing Our Faith: A Way of Life for a Searching People* (San Francisco: Jossey–Bass, 1997), 5.

[21]Craig Dykstra and Dorothy C. Bass, "A Theological Understanding of Christian Practices," in *Practicing Theology: Beliefs and Practices in Christian Life*, ed. Miroslav Volf and Dorothy C. Bass (Grand Rapids, Mich.: William B. Eerdmans, 2002), 21.

[22]http://www.practicingourfaith.com, accessed March 12, 2002.

[23]This phrase is taken from the first chapter of a unique book by James Hudnut–Beumler, *Generous Saints: Congregations Rethinking Ethics and Money* (Bethesda, Md.: Alban Institute, 1999), 1–14.

[24]David Tracy, *Plurality and Ambiguity: Hermeneutics, Religion, Hope* (San Francisco: Harper & Row, 1987), 9.

[25]*Catechism of the Catholic Church*, 399

[26]In the Roman Catholic church, one may choose to receive either the bread (body) or wine (blood), or both in the Eucharistic celebration.

[27]The term "emotional intelligence" was coined by Daniel Goleman. See his book, *Working with Emotional Intelligence* (New York: Bantam Books, 1997).

[28]I am indebted to the discussion of wonder and curiosity by Thomas F. Green in *The Activities of Teaching* (New York: McGraw Hill, 1971), 195–214.

[29]Philip H. Phenix, *Education and the Worship of God* (Philadelphia: The Westminster Press, 1966), 107.